MILITARY EXPENDITURE
THE POLITICAL ECONOMY OF
INTERNATIONAL SECURITY

STRATEGIC ISSUE PAPERS

The SIPRI series *Strategic Issue Papers* focuses on topical issues of significance for the future of international peace and security. Military expenditure is emerging as one of the central security and arms control issues of our time. SIPRI has therefore chosen *Military Expenditure: The Political Economy of International Security* as the fourth in the series. The studies address problems relating to arms reduction, the spread of arms, military and political strategy and the impact of technology on the conduct of peaceful East–West relations. The books are concise, with short production times so as to make a timely input into current debates.

sipri

SIPRI is an independent institute for research into problems of peace and conflict, especially those of arms control and disarmament. It was established in 1966 to commemorate Sweden's 150 years of unbroken peace.

The Institute is financed mainly by the Swedish Parliament. The staff, the Governing Board and the Scientific Council are international.

The Governing Board and the Scientific Council are not responsible for the views expressed in the publications of the Institute.

Governing Board

Ambassador Dr Inga Thorsson, Chairman (Sweden)
Professor Egon Bahr (Federal Republic of Germany)
Professor Francesco Calogero (Italy)
Dr Max Jakobson (Finland)
Professor Dr Karlheinz Lohs (German Democratic Republic)
Professor Emma Rothschild (United Kingdom)
Sir Brian Urquhart (United Kingdom)
The Director

Director

Dr Walther Stützle (Federal Republic of Germany)

sipri
Stockholm International Peace Research Institute

Pipers väg 28, S-171 73 Solna, Sweden
Cable: SIPRI
Telephone: 46 8/655 97 00
Telefax: 46 8/655 97 33

Military Expenditure
The Political Economy of International Security

Saadet Deger and Somnath Sen

Stockholm International Peace Research Institute

OXFORD UNIVERSITY PRESS
1990

Oxford University Press, Walton Street, Oxford OX2 6DP
Oxford New York Toronto
Delhi Bombay Calcutta Madras Karachi
Petaling Jaya Singapore Hong Kong Tokyo
Nairobi Dar es Salaam Cape Town
Melbourne Auckland
and associated companies in
Berlin Ibadan

Oxford is a trade mark of Oxford University Press

Published in the United States
by Oxford University Press, New York

© SIPRI 1990

British Library Cataloguing in Publication Data
Deger, Saadet, 1950–
Military expenditure: the political economy of
international security.—(Strategic issue papers)
1. Military equipment. Expenditure by governments
I. Title II. Sen Somnath III. Stockholm international
papers IV. Series
338.43623
ISBN 0–19–829141–8

Library of Congress Cataloging in Publication Data
Deger, Saadet, 1950–
Military expenditure: the political economy of international
security./Saadet Deger and Somnath Sen.
(Strategic issue papers)
Includes index.
1. Armed Forces—Appropriations and expenditures. 2. National
security—Economic Aspects. I. Sen, S. (Somnath) II. Title.
III. Series.
UA17.D44 1990 355.6'22—dc20 90–41690
ISBN 0–19–829141–8

Typeset and originated by Stockholm International Peace Research Institute
Printed and bound in Great Britain by
Biddles Ltd., Guildford and King's Lynn

Contents

Preface

World military expenditure, now approaching $1000 billion per year, reached unprecedentedly high levels during the 1980s. A major part was expended by the two superpowers, but other regional powers also contributed to the rise. The intensification of the 'cold war' in Europe during the early part of the decade was an important contributory factor in this process. Yet, the remarkable transformation that has taken place in the European peace and security order at the end of the 1980s leads us on to hope for a 'new world'.

Military Expenditure: The Political Economy of International Security documents this transformation and analyses, with numerous facts, figures, statistical data and estimates, the political and economic dimensions of world security. It utilizes defence spending as a prism through which the multi-dimensional aspects of security—military, political and economic—can be viewed. It discusses both the causes and the effects of military expenditure and the implications for international relations as well as domestic developments. It emphasizes the structural and systemic factors, arising out of technology and economics, that influence and motivate the arms race. But over and above these structural causes, this monograph shows that political will and vision must be the overriding factors in bringing about military spending limitations and successful arms control.

Dr Walther Stützle
SIPRI Director
May 1990

Acknowledgements

We are grateful to a number of people without whose help and co-operation this book would not have been completed. First and fore-most, Dr Walther Stützle initiated, encouraged and advised the research project from its inception. Madeleine Ströje Wilkens, Gunnel von Döbeln and Bibbi Henson have been a source of constant encouragement to our research in general. Connie Wall and Paul Claesson did a splendid job of editing the manuscript, and their excellence is self-evident. Cynthia Loo, as secretary to the World Military Expenditure programme, has accomplished the daunting task of typing the tables. Janet Meurling, and her dedicated library staff, helped us in finding background material. Carl-Gustaf Lagergren, Phitsamone Ljungqvist-Souvannavong and Fredrik Wetterqvist diligently assisted in the collection of data for appendix A. We thank them all.

Acronyms

ACDA	Arms Control and Disarmament Agency	CSCE	Conference on Security and Co-operation in Europe
ALCM	Air-launched cruise missile	CY	Calendar year
APC	Armoured personnel carrier	DIA	Defense Intelligence Agency
ASAT	Anti-satellite	DOD	Department of Defense
ASDF	Air Self Defense Forces	DOE	Department of Energy
ASEAN	Association of South-East Asian Nations	EC	European Community
		ECU	European Currency Unit
ATTU	Atlantic-to-the-Urals (zone)	EMU	Economic and Monetary Union
CATT	Conventional Arms Transfer Talks	FMS	Foreign Military Sales
		FY	Fiscal year
CBM	Confidence-building measure	FYP	Five-Year Plan
CBO	Congressional Budget Office	GDP	Gross domestic product
		GNP	Gross national product
CFE	Conventional Armed Forces in Europe (Negotiation)	ICBM	Intercontinental ballistic missile
CGE	Central government expenditure	IMF	International Monetary Fund
C^3I	Command, control, communications and intelligence	IRBM	Intermediate-range ballistic missile
		LDC	Less developed country
		LO	Low-observable
CIA	Central Intelligence Agency	MBFR	Mutual and Balance Force Reduction (Talks)
COCOM	Coordinating Committee (on Export Controls)	MBMW	Machine-building and metal-working
COMECON	Council for Mutual Economic Assistance	MBT	Main battle tank
		Milex	Military expenditure
CRS	Congressional Research Service	MIRV	Multiple independently targetable re-entry vehicle
CSBM	Confidence- and security-building measure	MND	Ministry of National Defence
CSCA	Conference on Security and Co-operation in Asia	MOD	Ministry of Defence

MOU	Memorandum of Understanding	SSBN	Nuclear-powered, ballistic-missile submarine
MTCR	Missile Technology Control Regime	SSM	Surface-to-surface missile
MTDP	Mid-Term Defense Plan	TASM	Tactical air-to-surface missile
NATO	North Atlantic Treaty Organization	TESD	Technological and economic structural disarmament
NCB	Nuclear, biological and chemical (weapons)		
NIC	Newly industrializing country	WEU	Western European Union
NMP	Net material product	WTO	Warsaw Treaty Organization (Warsaw Pact)
NSA	National Security Agency		
NSWTO	Non-Soviet WTO		
ODA	Official development assistance		
OECD	Organization for Economic Co-operation and Development		
O&M	Operation and maintenance		
OM&S	Operation, maintenance and support		
OMB	Office of Management and Budget		
PLA	People's Liberation Army		
R&D	Research and development		
RDT&E	Research, development, testing and evaluation		
SAM	Surface-to-air missile		
SDF	Self Defense Forces		
SDI	Strategic Defense Initiative		
SICBM	Small ICBM		
SII	Structural Impediments Initiative		
SLOC	Sea lanes of communcation		

1. Introduction: the end of a decade

I. Military expenditure and security

In terms of international security, the 1980s was in many respects a remarkable decade. It began with a competitive arms acquisition process, led by rapid increases in US military expenditure reversing the legacy of the post-Viet Nam War era. The Soviet Union responded, albeit slowly, constrained by an economic crisis. NATO as a whole, spurred by the US example, promulgated a 'rule' that defence spending be increased by 3 per cent per annum, making defence spending growth at high levels a policy objective (although in practice it was not consistently followed). The non-Soviet members of the Warsaw Treaty Organization also tried to stimulate military expenditure as a response to the arms buildup of the European NATO countries. The Third World intensified its weapon procurement programmes and increased its military expenditure. In this process it was stimulated by oil price increases, forced by ongoing and new conflicts and encouraged by the availability of credits to buy arms. The qualitative dimension of these financial resource inputs was an intensification of the arms dynamics, the introduction of new-generation weapon systems and the evolution of extremely sophisticated war-fighting technology.

In 1989 Europe experienced profound political change. The Berlin Wall was breached, symbolically and literally, and the rift between the two political systems that has divided the continent throughout the post-war era tended to close. The future of the two alliances was called into question. It became increasingly clear that war was no longer a major political option in Europe. A new President in the United States faced increasing budgetary problems in sorting out defence priorities. The Soviet Union embarked, probably for the first time in 20 years, on a major re-allocation of resources from the military to the civilian sector. Arms control negotiations looked increasingly as if they were close to success. The Third World was more concerned with economic than with military security. Political factors coalesced with the forces of technological and economic structural disarmament, raising hopes for significant reductions in world military expenditure.

Performance has yet to match up to promises, however. The actual reduction of world military expenditure (after adjustments for inflation) between 1988 and 1989 was modest—slightly less than 2 per cent according to preliminary SIPRI estimates. In the area of defence spending most governments seemed to be satisfied to follow a policy of 'wait and see'. The rapid increases of the early 1980s have disappeared, but deep cuts in defence spending are still not visible, nor are the rewards of the current disarmament process. Military expenditure is now in a stable and gentle decline, probably in anticipation of successful and verifiable arms control negotiations.

Military expenditure is a measure or a metric which can be used to explain the various dimensions of international security—military, political and economic. It also links domestic developments to foreign policy concerns, a linkage which will become more important in the future. A study of the causes and effects of military expenditure will therefore throw light on many facets of the security relations between—as well as within—states. This book is an attempt to provide documentary evidence on the evolution of defence spending over the 1980s and to analyse the political economy aspects of that evolution. The time period is particularly relevant since it represents a sort of crossroads in post-World War II history. In addition to looking at aggregate defence spending, the allocation structure, in terms of personnel, procurement, research and development (R&D), is also analysed in some detail, to reveal interesting facets of military and foreign policy behaviour as well as the economic effects of defence expansion and limitation. The discussion of military spending is therefore related to budgetary allocations, procurement policy, economic change and reforms, industrial organization, research strategy as well as foreign policy objectives.

There are a number of reasons why a study of military expenditure (and its allocation) is important in the context of analysing national security and foreign policy objectives.

1. It is an aggregate measure of defence resource input—and, under well-specified input–output relationships, of military capability—that is easy to understand and to use as a means of comparison.

2. Its allocation over time into various component parts gives an indication of force structure and military capability trends.

3. Its growth indicates the preferences and perceptions of policy makers.

4. Its expansion, within a dyadic framework, is often an indicator of an arms race with implications for conflicts and wars.

5. It measures economic costs for a weak economy and shows how vulnerable a country can be from the point of view of non-military threats to security. This may be important in the context of stability.

6. It can be used by governments, particularly in countries which are in opposition to each other, to demonstrate how belligerent or benign the spender is.

7. It is most often utilized as an indicator of alliance burden-sharing and is a measure (adjusted for scale and size) for allocating 'fair' shares.

8. It can be used by governments to convince domestic political groups of the necessity to increase military expenditure. A classic example of this is the Reagan Administration's justification for the US defence buildup in the 1980s, that is, that the Soviet Union had far outstripped the United States in military expenditure during the previous decade and that the gap needed to be narrowed.

9. Its long-term economic effects (as distinct from short-term costs), if adverse, could affect the spending country's security.

II. The rise and fall of military expenditure

In his State of the Union message in 1981, President Ronald Reagan claimed that the Soviet Union had in the 1970s spent $300 billion more than the United States on defence. The dubious method used to calculate that figure notwithstanding, the President sought to justify the largest peacetime expansion ever of US military spending using Soviet defence expenditures. The so called 'military expenditure' gap was invoked to allow rapid increases in defence spending. In addition, there was the alleged 'window of vulnerability' by which a Soviet nuclear first strike could destroy US land-based ICBMs. Such fears prompted the expensive search for space-based defensive strategic weapons leading on to the Strategic Defense Initiative. Finally, there was a belief that the traditionally overwhelming US naval superiority was diminishing, inspiring the decision, later amended, to build a '600 ship navy'.[1]

The Carter Administration had already started a modest buildup of US military capability after the reductions in the post-Viet Nam War era. What characterized the expansion under President Reagan was the rapidity of the increase and the technological sophistication (implied by the growth of military R&D) that went with it. According to SIPRI data, between 1980 and 1985 US military spending grew by 7 per cent in real terms (after adjusting for inflation). The military burden, defined as the proportion of defence spending in GDP, rose from slightly less than 5 per cent to 6.7 per cent in 1980–86.

There is some evidence of a slow-down in Soviet defence spending in the late Brezhnev period. In the early 1980s Soviet defence spending growth was low, although the military burden was more than double that of the United States. In response to US military growth the USSR followed a classic arms race action–reaction pattern and stepped up its own expansion plans. Although Soviet measures of GNP are controversial, it is possible that defence spending growth outstripped that of national product so that the military share rose in the first half of the 1980s from its already high level. According to some analysts, this caused an excessive burden to the economy.

Both European NATO and non-Soviet WTO countries responded to the example set by their respective leading allies, although their response to arms expansion was more muted. Since world military expenditure is highly concentrated with more than three-fourths of the global total emanating from the two alliances, the aggregate trend was firmly upwards. Taken as a whole, the Third World countries also rapidly increased their military spending, mainly as a result of wars and oil revenues.

The decline and fall of military expenditure began in the latter part of the 1980s, initially prompted by structural factors such as excessive cost increases but later prompted by the possibilities for arms control through negotiations. As mentioned above, the reduction in world military expenditure has been modest, never falling by more than 2 per cent per annum during the two years 1987–88 and 1988–89, when such reductions took place. It must be stressed that the decline is taking place from very high levels, implying that with such modest

[1] Kaufmann, W. W. and Korb, L. J., *The 1990 Defense Budget* (Brookings Institution, Washington, DC, 1989).

rates it might take many years simply to return to the defence spending level of 1980. Unless there is a dramatic shift in political perceptions, and the technological arms dynamic is put into reverse gear, military expenditure limitations will not be significant in the short run.

III. Military expenditure limitations

There is a central unifying principle that in this study binds together, within a well-specified framework, the description of events and trends. In the period in question, essentially two types of force are at work producing pressure on defence spending and creating a sort of 'scissors crisis' for the armed forces. One is based on technological factors, such as the level of sophistication required for modern-warfare weapons, the utilization of emerging technology or the need to use space programmes for strategic defence. In a confrontational world this technological input has to be used, simply 'because it's there'. When 'invention becomes the mother of necessity', however, more questions will be asked and new programmes more closely evaluated before decisions are made regarding procurement or even research, development, testing and evaluation (RDT&E). Closely related is the consideration of cost and budgetary constraints which puts a strict upper limit on what the government and society can afford. Even for the richest countries of the world, defence spending and the cost of national security are no longer beyond question.

These technological and economic constraints are structural in nature and are in the long term beyond the control of individual policy makers. Taken together, this force of technological and economic structural disarmament (TESD) will produce some limitations on weapon acquisition and generate unilateral arms control. Even for conventional weapons, the costs involved in their use on modern societies are simply too horrifying to contemplate. The speed at which modernization programmes have been implemented in recent years all over the world is breathtaking and will now stop because of the inertia generated by TESD. Clearly, being systemic by nature, its impact will be slow and long-term.

The second major force arises out of the invigorated arms control process, the greater degree of confidence- and security-building measures (CSBMs) among the major powers, the profound political and economic changes taking place in Europe and a heightened awareness that military conflict may no longer be a political option, particularly in democratic societies in which internal prosperity by necessity is given priority over external conflict. The force generated by political will, to reduce conflicts and further the peace process, is central to all aspects of arms control and concomitant military expenditure limitations. To be meaningful, however, it requires a willingness to accept reductions in military spending and deployment that in the immediate term may be seen as inexpedient. Soviet President Mikhail Gorbachev aside, few political leaders have cut the Gordian knot of tangled arms control negotiations by proposing, and effecting, significant unilateral force reductions below negotiated levels.

A question remains, however. Is there actually any need to consider military expenditure reductions, particularly within the context of arms control? As Abraham Becker succinctly puts it: 'If it is men and weapons that constitute the threat to peace, why be concerned with dollars and roubles?'[2] The history of arms control negotiations and disarmament measures has been exclusively concerned with quantitative restrictions and reductions in military assets and forces. It is interesting to note that the first major initiative on military spending cuts was proposed as early as 1899, by Czarist Russia in the Hague Peace Conference. There are a number of reasons why defence expenditure reductions are related to successful arms control measures even though they may be difficult to monitor, verify and even implement.

1. Explicitly limiting defence budgets may resolve the quantity/quality paradox that is inherent in arms control. Physical constraints on military stocks do not guarantee the reductions in capability that are needed to produce a peaceful environment. Arms control and modernization often go hand in hand, and quantity reductions may at the same time lead to quality increases. As shown in this book, R&D spending has been maintained by the major powers even when they have tried to implement reductions in assets or programmes. This produces pressure to have compensating increases in areas of weapon procurement not subject to control.

[2] Becker, A. S., *Military Expenditure Limitation for Arms Control: Problems and Prospects* (Ballinger: Cambridge, Mass., 1977), p. 2.

2. Financial restrictions cover all possible military activities while physical limitations can only be relevant to certain areas. Traditional arms control, for example, can never affect the evolution of R&D and technological progress. On the other hand, defence spending cuts can do so if necessary.

3. Monetary measures of arms control allow governments a large degree of flexibility to tailor reductions to their specific security needs determined by national and geographic needs. The decision to have conscripts or volunteers, or alternatively to spend more on one service branch or another depending on military threats, can be adjusted within the overall financial constraints.

Arms control considerations aside, reduction of the costs of defence, particularly in a period of *détente* as well as budgetary pressures, is in itself a laudable purpose. This is particularly true when there are major social and economic needs which cannot be met by the government subject to high security expenditures. Saving resources is particularly important for poor developing countries—and it is certainly not unimportant for advanced industrial nations. The case of the USSR, in which resources are transferred from the military to the civil economy, is discussed in chapter 6. Even for the USA, high military consumption has been a burden to the Government, which particularly during the 1980s has been troubled by alarmingly high budget deficits as well as an inability of the economy to save more rather than borrowing from abroad, contributing to an equally high trade deficit.

To sum up, the aim of this book is to document events central to, and to identify the forces behind, military expenditure expansion and reductions during the 1980s. The book expands substantially upon chapters 5 and 6 by the present authors in the *SIPRI Yearbook 1990*. It is important to stress that most of the research presented in this monograph was completed by the end of 1989. It is essential to provide the date of documentation since some conclusions may become irrelevant at a time of fundamental change in the political and economic environment that conditions international security. The decade of the 1980s is of particular interest since it saw unprecedented expansion of global resources allocated to the military sector. At the same time, the political changes brought about in the last year of the decade raise hopes for a qualitative transformation of the international military system by the end of the millenium.

2. European NATO: change or continuity?

I. The 40th year

NATO celebrated its 40th anniversary in 1989 with what seemed to be a middle age crisis. The arms control process and the rapid pace of political change in Europe produced different types of challenge. The former requires planning for weapon reductions, while NATO's objective for the past four decades has been weapon accumulation. The latter questions the very rationale for NATO and suggests that the predominantly military alliance must now become a more political grouping.

From the late 1970s through the 1980s, the NATO Defence Planning Committee called for a real increase of military expenditure by 3 per cent per annum. Few countries have strictly adhered to this suggested 'rule'. However, the call was not purely symbolic. Military expenditure did rise substantially for most countries, at least until 1986–87, although the lion's share of this increase was taken up by the USA. Among the major European NATO member states, the following per annum growth in defence spending was noted between 1980 and the 'peak' year (1986 or 1987) for the respective countries: 1.7 per cent for France; 1.1 per cent for the Federal Republic of Germany; 1 per cent for the Netherlands; 2.6 per cent for Spain; and 2.6 per cent for the UK. Italian military spending rose consistently throughout the decade, at a rate of 4.4 per cent per year in 1980–89. Expenditure in the smaller countries in the southern flank, Greece and Turkey, also increased rapidly, at least until the late 1980s.

Even as late as June 1989, the need for an annual 3 per cent increase in defence spending was reiterated at the annual NATO Defence Planning Committee meeting. Only in 1990, in response to the disintegration of the WTO, was this target finally abandoned. It is now clear that military spending increases are out of the question. The issue at present is the extent of the decline and how rapidly adjustments in forces and assets will take place. Current evidence suggests that the cuts will be slow and cautious, but political changes might speed up the process dramatically.

The Final Communiqué of the May 1990 NATO Defence Planning Committee states:

We can now begin to reap the benefits of the greatly improved climate in East/West relations. As a first step, we have concluded that the general target, first agreed in 1977, of annual real increases in defence expenditure of the order of 3% is no longer appropriate, although expenditure plans will continue to need to reflect particular national circumstances. The need to maintain a credible and effective defence posture will remain the basis for determining the resources for collective defence. As a result of a CFE Treaty, some reduction in overall defence expenditure can be expected. However, these savings will be partly offset by costs associated with the implementation of the treaty, e.g. the costs of destruction, verification and the necessary restructuring of our forces. In the longer term, further reduction in overall defence expenditure may be possible through a continuation of the arms control process.[1]

Precisely for the reasons mentioned above—costs of reorganization, treaty verification and asset destruction—large savings in budgets may not be yet forthcoming. Further, NATO clearly recognizes that the WTO as a whole is no longer a credible threat, and arms control treaty implementation 'will virtually eliminate the possibility of a surprise attack on NATO'.[2] Yet, it seems that a sort of insurance policy is still required, and major changes, which could produce large reductions in defence spending, will not occur in the short term. If a US force withdrawal requires some replacements, then more money will have to be spent by European NATO. As shown in chapter 6, the unilateral response of the WTO countries has been much stronger, and sizeable cuts have already been made.

One final point needs to be stressed. The alliance ceilings so far proposed by NATO at the Vienna CFE Negotiation imply relatively modest reductions of assets. Deep cuts will be forthcoming only in future CFE agreements, but not in the current one expected to be signed in 1990. The latest data available at the time of writing, from Round VII of the CFE Negotiation in May, show that the proposed ceilings for the ATTU (Atlantic-to-the-Urals) zone are still quite close

---

[1] *Atlantic News*, Brussels, no. 2226 (24 May 1990), p. 2 of the Annex.
[2] See note 1.

to current holdings.[3] According to the NATO position, the following reductions in assets are envisaged for the Alliance: tanks, from 24 429 to 20 000 (a cut of 18 per cent); ACVs, from 29 680 to 30 000 (a marginal increase); artillery, from 18 504 to 16 500 (a cut of 11 per cent); and aircraft, from 6180 to 5200 (a reduction of 16 per cent). This implies a cut of 10–15 per cent, in aggregate, for NATO weapon stocks. There can be no doubt that the establishment of fixed ceilings is a very positive step indeed towards stopping the *growth* of arms acquisition and must have positive implications for arms control and even future disarmament. However, the requirements for replacement procurement, O&M, support costs as well as technological modernization all remain at current levels. Ultimately, the only way out of the cycle of arms races is to have deep cuts.

II. The burden-sharing debate

Throughout the 1980s a debate went on regarding the burden-sharing of costs and responsibilities between the twin pillars of NATO—the USA and European members of the Atlantic alliance. Although NATO officially maintained a firm line that the burden was shared equitably, political discussions in the USA were particularly critical of the so-called 'free rider' behaviour of European countries. As the political changes of 1989 unfolded, the criticisms became muted and possibly irrelevant since burden-shedding became more relevant than burden-sharing. The analysis therefore could seem only academic here. Yet, there are two fundamental reasons why it is important to understand the concepts and discuss the implications of sharing costs in an alliance. First, lessons can be learned from historical experience of how the burden of aggregate defence was allocated among the members. Second, if the USA does pull out of Europe in the future and a federal security structure is imposed on the continent, then the burden-sharing debate will crop up again, but this time among the European members alone, of how best to apportion collective security expenditures. The analysis below, although put in an historical setting, may provide some answers to the future problem.

---

[3] Calculations based on basic data in *Vienna Fax: News and Analysis*, from the Vienna Negotiation on Conventional Armed Forces in Europe and Confidence- and Security-Building Measures, no. 18 (18 May 1990), p. 2.

As the economic problems emanating from US military expenditures and concomitant budget deficits have increased, so also was there an increasing US call for a more equitable participation by the European pillar of NATO towards its own defence. The distribution of the economic costs of NATO towards Europe and away from the USA was considered at one time to be a prime factor in trans-Atlantic security relationships. The year 1988 saw a particularly strident call from US sources, at all levels, towards a greater economic contribution by the European allies towards the common defence. As a former National Security Adviser summed it up: 'Surely, 374 million Europeans with an aggregate economy of $3.5 trillion should not need to depend for their defense as heavily as they do on 241 million Americans with an economy of $4 trillion—against an opponent with [a population of] 275 million and a GNP of only $1.9 trillion'.[4] This issue has been called the burden-sharing debate and needs to be analysed in some detail.

Although the US Administration has always been committed to its contribution towards NATO defence in Europe, and little change is expected for the Bush Administration years, there were at least three important opinion-making groups which kept the debate at the forefront during the 1980s. The first was the academic community. Its discussions, although counter-factual and asking 'what if' questions, were the most wide-ranging; they stretched at the one end from asking whether the USA still considers itself as a European power, to the other extreme, asking whether the country has already begun its decline from its position as a global imperial power.[5] More influential, although narrower in scope, were the media, which started speculating about a US force withdrawal in the near future;[6] but the maximum immediate impact came from Congress, where important sections voiced grave reservations about European contributions to NATO.[7]

---

[4] Brzezinski, Z., reported in J. Barry and R. Watson, 'Can Europe stand on its own feet?', *Newsweek*, 7 Dec. 1987, p. 32.

[5] For an exposition, see Hunter, R. E., 'Will the United States remain a European power?', *Survival*, vol. 30, no. 3 (May/June 1988), pp. 201–31. A much more general historical perspective on related questions of imperial power can be found in Kennedy, P., *The Rise and Fall of the Great Powers: Economic Change and Military Conflict from 1500 to 2000* (Random House: New York, 1987).

[6] Safire, W., 'The European pillar', *New York Times*, 7 Apr. 1988.

[7] Symptomatic of congressional concern at US cost escalations for European security needs is the bill proposed by Rep. Jack Davis which sought to penalize countries which do not compensate the USA when the dollar falls and it becomes more expensive to pay for overseas expenditures. Senate discussions on the FY 1989 defence budget also mentioned burden-sharing; see *International Herald Tribune*, 12 Aug. 1988. The Senate wanted new restrictions

The most authoritative evidence on the US (Congress') point of view came in the form of the report of the Defense Burdensharing Panel of the Committee on Armed Services, House of Representatives. It stated its case dramatically:

In 1988, concerns about the Federal deficit, the trade imbalance, high Federal spending generally and high defence spending specifically have ignited a national debate about our future defense needs and a reassessment of US global military commitments. Many Americans feel that we are competing 100 per cent *militarily* with the Soviets and 100 per cent *economically* with our defense allies. Some have said that the United States has incurred all the burdens of empire and few, if any, of the benefits.[8]

The Report presented a number of arguments which seemed to claim that European NATO countries are paying a disproportionately low share of Alliance costs; hence they are not contributing a 'fair' share of the total burden. However, some fundamental theoretical and empirical points were not clearly enunciated, and it is worth noting the implications of the analysis and (possible) allegations.

NATO members, as part of a 'club', enjoy the benefits of collective security and are required to pay a cost—the so-called burden-sharing. However, since the benefits of deterrence, security and peace are collective in nature (no one can be excluded, in principle, from enjoying them, independent of payment), this is a classic case of a public good. Apportioning the cost of providing the public good can be done either in terms of the benefits received (the benefit approach) or in terms of the ability of the recipients to pay (the ability-to-pay approach).

It is safe to claim that from the point of view of the benefit approach the USA should pay the maximum since its strategic, political and economic stakes are the highest in the Alliance. Its rewards are twofold: they encompass both the national and international dimensions. The twin pillars of NATO are North America and Europe. The former relates to US national concerns—the defence of its homeland. The latter relates to the United States as a global power and *a fortiori* as a European power. It is doubtful that, if it did not have an European presence, the USA would be still considered the

on overseas spending; but more important, it mandated a special envoy to negotiate the issue with the Europeans.

[8] *Report of the Defense Burdensharing Panel of the Committee on Armed Services, US House of Representatives* (US Government Printing Office: Washington, DC, Aug. 1988), pp. 2–3.

most important superpower in the world. No other ally within NATO aspires to be a world power, in terms of politico-economic and military strengths, as much as the USA; but if its flag does not fly over Europe the loss of global credibility will be immense.

In terms of the ability-to-pay approach as well, the USA should pay the most since its overall economy is much the largest within NATO. In terms of both aggregate national output and resource endowment (including land area and population), it is the largest economy in the Alliance, so it is not surprising that its contribution is the highest.

The fact that the trans-Atlantic relation is not a simple one-way street and the US economy gains a lot from the partnership is exemplified by the defence trade balance between the USA and European NATO. At a time of unprecedented overall trade deficit and loss of competitiveness of US industries, the defence sector shows a healthy trade surplus with Europe (going against the general trend). In FY 1983 the USA sold eight times more defence products than it bought from Europe. Although this ratio is going down, it still remains significantly in favour of the USA. For example, in FY 1986 Europe sold $1999 million of weapons but bought a total worth $3247 million; the US trade surplus was of the order of $1248 million.[9]

A more detailed quantitative breakdown of what Europe actually provides on the continent, rather than a simple financial account, is revealing. A Euro-group ministerial statement[10] and the NATO Defence Planning Committee Report[11] claimed that the European allies, even excluding France and Spain, provided around 1988 an overwhelming proportion of NATO's operational forces and weapons for European defence: 95 per cent of the divisions; 90 per cent of the manpower; 90 per cent of the artillery; 80 per cent of the tanks; 80 per cent of the combat aircraft; 65 per cent of the major warships; 70 per cent of submarines; and most of the mine countermeasure vessels. By any criterion, European NATO's capability input to the Alliance is substantial.

---

[9] Maroni, A., 'US perspectives on the economic costs and benefits of a withdrawal of US troops and facilities from Europe', in ed. J. M. O. Sharp, SIPRI, *Europe After an American Withdrawal: Economic and Military Issues* (Oxford University Press: Oxford, 1990), chapter 3.

[10] The Euro-group was founded in 1968 to propagate and ensure that the European contribution to NATO is appropriate. This statement was published on its 20th anniversary. Quoted from *NATO's Sixteen Nations*, June 1988, p. 41.

[11] *Enhancing Alliance Collective Security: Shared Roles, Risks and Responsibility in the Alliance*, Report by NATO's Defence Planning Committee, Dec. 1988.

Table 2.1. Mobilizable defence personnel of selected NATO countries as a share of the labour force, 1988 projections

Figures are percentages.

Country	1988 projection
Belgium	5.26
Denmark	3.96
FRG	5.33
Greece	11.35
Italy	2.89
Netherlands	4.97
Norway	11.19
Portugal	6.12
Spain	5.39
Turkey	5.24
UK	2.33
USA (total)	3.69
USA (excl. European forces)	3.15

Sources: *NATO Defence Planning Committee Report*, Dec. 1988; authors' calculations.

Another input that is vital is personnel. To analyse capability, it is essential to consider total mobilization during wartime since this is the crucial indicator of strategic preparedness. Unfortunately, the actual numbers mean little, since countries cannot be compared due to variations in size. One relative measure of the human input that a nation makes to its defence effort is the share of the total *mobilizable* force (active military manpower, civilian personnel in the defence sector and reserves) in its total labour force (the economically active population). Table 2.1 gives figures for this percentage share in 1988 for 12 of the 16 NATO countries. In a sense this measures the labour 'burden' or the share of the labour force which will be diverted to the military from its most productive functions for the economy. Here, the performance of European NATO is generally superior to that of the United States.

However, the Panel tried to make a strong case in favour of the US contribution by citing the country's military expenditure as a proportion of GDP—technically called the *defence burden*. For the USA this has been, in recent years, above 6 per cent, while the allies have generally had a much lower figure. However, this argument obfuscates two major empirical issues. First, it is not always clear how much US defence spending is exclusively for NATO. The aggregate becomes meaningless since it includes global commitments, national protection as well as European defence. Unless these allocations are well specified, the NATO or European component cannot be meaningfully compared. Second, the use of a non-conscript or professional armed force tends to raise the personnel costs and military expenditure for the USA.

It has been reported that, for the early to mid-1980s, around 52–58 per cent of US defence spending was for the benefit of NATO.[12] The House Report gives a figure of 60 per cent, but this includes substantial numbers of forces and equipment deployed in the USA for reinforcements in the European theatre in case of war. Hence, they are dual-capable; essentially these can be used also for purely national defence. A much smaller share, of around 15 per cent of annual US military spending, is thought to be required to cover the following costs for NATO: all direct costs of deploying US forces in Europe; allocated costs of new equipment as well as training, logistics and R&D; and DOD administration expenses.[13] If these lower and upper limits, 15 per cent and 60 per cent, are considered, then the 6 per cent aggregate US military burden comes down to only around 0.9 and 3.6 per cent, respectively, as the share of military expenditure (in GDP) devoted to NATO.

The second issue is equally important. A crucial factor that needs to be considered in the burden-sharing debate is that most European allies (except the UK) use conscripts, rather than volunteers paid at the market wage, to maintain their armed forces. Thus the personnel cost is kept down at artificially low levels so that the defence burden does not reflect the true cost to the country. This is particularly true at a time of profound demographic changes causing skilled labour shortages; conscripts are essentially diverted from the civilian sectors with concomitant implicit losses to the economy. This opportunity cost must be included in any proper assessment of what the 'true' military burden actually is. Alternatively, countries which opt for a paid volunteer army are allocating resources optimally since the soldiers are paid according to their productivity in a job that they wish

---

[12] Knorr, K., 'Burden sharing in NATO: aspects of US policy', *Orbis*, autumn 1985, p. 530.
[13] See note 9.

Table 2.2. Military expenditure as a share of GDP, selected NATO countries with volunteer armed forces, 1985–88

Figures are percentages.

Country	1985 Actual	1985 Est.	1986 Actual	1986 Est.	1987 Actual	1987 Est.	1988 Actual	1988 Est.
Belgium	3.0	3.6	3.0	3.4	2.9	3.4	2.7	3.3
Denmark	2.2	2.4	2.0	2.2	2.1	2.3	2.2	..
France	4.0	4.4	3.9	4.3	4.0	4.3	3.8	4.1
FRG	3.2	3.6	3.1	3.4	3.1	3.5	2.9	3.4
Greece	7.0	8.9	6.2	7.9	6.3	7.9	6.4	7.4
Italy	2.3	2.8	2.2	2.8	2.4	3.1	2.5	..
Netherlands	3.1	3.5	3.1	3.5	3.1	3.4	3.0	..
Norway	3.1	3.7	3.1	3.8	3.3	4.1	3.2	..
Portugal	3.1	3.8	3.2	n.a.	3.1	n.a.	3.2	..
Spain	2.4	2.9	2.2	2.7	2.4	2.9	2.1	..
Turkey	4.5	5.9	4.8	6.3	4.2	5.8	3.8	..
UK	5.1	5.2	4.9	5.0	4.8	4.7	4.3	4.5
USA lower[a]	n.a.	1.0	n.a.	1.0	n.a.	1.0	n.a.	0.9
USA upper[a]	n.a.	4.0	n.a.	4.0	n.a.	3.9	n.a.	3.7

[a] US ratios relate to expenditures in connection with NATO. Figures not applicable (n.a.) for the USA are those related to actual US defence expenditure.

Source: Authors' calculations.

to have. In addition, there are political costs to the compulsory conscript system since it is generally unpopular.

Table 2.2 gives the defence burden for European NATO countries which rely on conscription. A 'what if' calculation is made: What would the share of military expenditure be if the conscripts are paid a market wage? These estimated defence burdens are reported for 1985–88 and compared with the actual figures which are given in the adjacent columns. Since details of rank and force structures are not known for all the countries concerned, a simplifying assumption has been made: it is assumed that each conscript is paid the average annual industrial wage. Where data for wages are not available, per capita GDP is used to cost each conscripted recruit. In general, military personnel tend to be paid better than industrial workers, so these calculated figures should be considered as underestimates. For the sake of comparison, actual figures for the UK are also provided. In the last two rows, the contribution of the USA towards NATO is considered and the relevant defence burden calculated using the two limits mentioned above.

As table 2.2 shows, the alleged large disparity between US and European defence burdens tends to disappear. The bigger countries, France and the UK, tend to have a larger share of defence spending in GDP than the upper limit of the USA; so do the poorer countries Greece and Turkey. All European countries have a higher defence burden compared to the lower US limit. The FRG data presented here only cost the conscripts, but the FRG also spends a large amount on the military security of Berlin which is not included in the NATO definition of defence expenditures and is not counted in the calculations here. However, when these costs are included, the FRG defence burden exceeds significantly the maximum US limit for NATO-related expenditures. Between 1983 and 1988, the military burden of the FRG varied between 3 and 3.3 per cent. However, under the hypothesized scenario with volunteer armed forces and Berlin costs added, the burden would have varied from 4.2 to 4.6 per cent.

The conclusion is inescapable: in terms of direct financial spending, European NATO countries tend to have lower defence burdens relative to the United States. This is the core of the burden-sharing critique. However, once direct and indirect (opportunity) costs are included, and US NATO commitments are taken into account, it is clear that the European countries generally have a higher share of military expenditure in GDP. It is but fair to make the latter comparison since aggregate US military spending includes operations with which NATO cannot be directly concerned. What must really be costed is US *NATO*-related spending only, since the concern is one of *NATO* burden-sharing. Within this framework the burden seems to be equitable and fair on a national basis.

Finally, there is one perspective regarding 'bring the boys back home' that cannot be overlooked. There are around 325 000 US servicemen in Europe, and more than one-third will be withdrawn under the Bush proposal for the CFE agreement. It is clear that if there is to be any budgetary impact then these forces cannot be kept in the armed forces any longer and will become unemployed. The implications for US unemployment must therefore also be considered.

For analytical exposition, the extreme case can be considered of what will happen if all US forces are removed from Europe and released from the services. The unemployment rate would rise to 6.5 per cent. In addition, if substantial budgetary cuts are made, not only personnel but also procurement will be affected. US arms industrial output will also be seriously affected, and all these factors will lead to retrenchment and substantial increases in defence-related job losses. Once again the implications for US unemployment could be vital. Consider again the extreme case in which 60 per cent of the US budget is used for NATO purposes. If this is totally eliminated, then the impact on defence industrial employment will be extremely serious. A 60 per cent reduction of procurement would mean that the aggregate US unemployment rate would become 8.1 per cent; this implies a proportionate increase of 30 per cent of the relevant rate.[14] Such a high increase would be totally unacceptable from a political point of view.

These counter-factual analyses are indicative of the basic propositions that are central to the burden-sharing debate. In terms of security, global power and a predominant role in international relations, the US contribution to the Alliance cost is not excessive. But even if the case is considered from a purely economic cost–benefit perspective, US gains are substantial in terms of defence industrial output, trade and employment generation. In addition, Europe does contribute a high share of the total force structure and overall cost. If the indirect and opportunity costs are all accounted for, the contribution of the European pillar is substantial. Taking even a narrow measure such as the share of military expenditure in GDP, the military burden of many European countries exceeds that of the USA, where the latter's NATO contributions are concerned.

In a sense this question of *burden-sharing* has been relatively futile, particularly if one considers the above analysis. What the main concern should have been is that of *burden-shedding* rather than burden-sharing. In the light of the proposed transformation in global security perceptions, the acrimonious debate on who should pay what has now ended.

[14] All estimates have been made for FY 1988 forecasts as of Apr. 1988. The basic data are from the US Defense Budget; see *National Defense Budget Estimates for FY 1988/1989* (Office of the Assistant Secretary of Defense (Comptroller): Washington, DC, 1988).

III. Major weapon procurement

Since the current arms control negotiations will have the maximum impact on procurement spending on *major* weapon acquisition, the analysis of that process assumes greater importance. SIPRI has estimated comprehensive 10-year time series data for equipment expenditures (for CYs 1980–89) for all NATO countries.[15] These are provided in current prices, local currencies (table 2.3) as well as in constant-price 1988 US dollars (table 2.4). The estimates have been based on raw data provided by NATO, using the NATO definition, which differs substantially from what is usually called 'procurement' in national defence budgets. Only in the case of France have estimates been made from national sources,[16] since French forces are not integrated with those of the rest of NATO. The trend for France, however, is consistent and comparable with all other countries.

For the whole of NATO, aggregate cumulative equipment expenditure for major weapons amounted to $860 billion (in constant 1988 prices and exchange-rates) over the 1980s. Of this amount, the USA accounted for $635 billion and European NATO for $208 billion. From 1980 to the peak year 1987, expenditures rose continuously in real terms. After 1987 they began to fall. In the 1980–87 period major procurement spending increased by 7.7 per cent per year for NATO, 10.2 per cent per year for the USA and 3.1 per cent per year for the European NATO countries. In comparison, the fall from 1987 to 1989 was modest: in this period major equipment expenditures declined by 4 per cent per year for NATO, 4.5 per cent per year for the USA and 1.7 per cent for the European NATO countries.

Forecasts have also shown how long it would take from 1989 for procurement spending to reach the 1980 level if the rate of reductions over 1987–89 are carried on into the future. European NATO would need until the year 2000 to attain the annual level of equipment spending (in constant prices) it had in 1980. In other words, it would take more than 10 years of continuous reduction at the present rate simply to reach the level of expenditure that was prevalent at the beginning of the decade.

[15] These data first appeared in SIPRI, *SIPRI Yearbook 1990: World Armaments and Disarmament* (Oxford University Press: Oxford, 1990), chapter 5.

[16] For French budget data, see French Ministry of Defence, *Projet de loi de Finances pour 1989* (Government Printer: Paris, 1988).

Table 2.3. NATO major weapon procurement expenditure, in local currency, 1980–89

Figures are in local currency, current prices.

		1980	1981	1982	1983	1984	1985	1986	1987	1988	1989
North America											
Canada	m. dollars	847	1 000	1 332	1 688	1 971	1 941	2 140	2 434	2 486	2 350
USA	m. dollars	28 076	34 487	42 028	50 202	58 328	66 348	72 525	76 362	71 808	75 081
Europe											
Belgium	m. francs	16 669	17 596	17 969	18 853	18 363	18311	19 618	20 360	18 078	14 896
Denmark	m. kroner	1 468	1 803	1 960	2 075	2 048	1 841	1 867	2 182	2 249	2 435
France	m. francs	23 786	29 444	34 637	39 772	42 216	46 492	49 664	55 943	56 564	59 773
FR Germany	m. D. marks	7 181	9 029	9 437	9 774	9 450	8 680	9 561	9 326	8 938	9 047
Greece	m. drachmas	18 231	29 287	29 966	30 741	41 604	46 687	53 477	67 605	112 141	116 230
Italy	b. lire	1 436	1 707	2 046	2 664	2 843	3 494	3 693	4 900	5 451	5 903
Luxembourg	m. francs	28	31	44	36	36	91	74	106	89	135
Netherlands	m. guilders	1 896	2 135	2 444	2 794	3 012	3 019	2 661	2 359	2 713	2 608
Norway	m. kroner	1 591	1 799	2 147	2 615	2 297	3 846	3 303	3 784	4 018	6 293
Portugal	m. escudos	2 650	3 375	3 318	3 761	4 416	3 675	8 818	16 088	20 356	27 837
Spain	m. pesetas	69 033	70 966	84 291	116 707	170 745	113 380	168 812	210 633	172 918	134 089
Turkey	b. lira	87	29	48	56	105	168	334	553	853	1 233
UK	m. pounds	2 901	3 218	3 545	4 122	4 629	4 907	4 762	4 744	4 904	4 759

Sources: NATO publications; authors' calculations. Figures for France are based on national data.

Table 2.4. NATO and EC major weapon procurement expenditure, in US dollars, 1980–89

Figures are in US $m., at constant (1988) prices.

	1980	1981	1982	1983	1984	1985	1986	1987	1988	1989
North America										
Canada	1 114	1 169	1 405	1 683	1 883	1 784	1 887	2 058	2 020	1 860
USA	40 281	44 854	51 493	59 581	66 359	72 917	78 219	79 396	71 808	71 813
Europe										
Belgium	663	650	611	595	545	518	548	560	492	394
Denmark	360	396	390	386	359	308	301	339	334	346
France	6 863	7 490	7 878	8 255	8 151	8 492	8 850	9 648	9 496	9 722
FR Germany	5 003	5 919	5 879	5 892	5 563	5 002	5 520	5 369	5 089	4 998
Greece	534	689	583	497	569	535	498	541	790	733
Italy	2 482	2 469	2 540	2 883	2 778	3 128	3 122	3 954	4 188	4 285
Luxembourg	1.1	1.1	1.5	1.1	1.0	2.5	2.0	2.9	2.4	3.6
Netherlands	1 178	1 243	1 344	1 494	1 560	1 523	1 346	1 202	1 373	1 308
Norway	468	465	499	560	463	734	588	620	617	924
Portugal	70	74	59	54	49	34	73	123	141	174
Spain	1 265	1 135	1 180	1 456	1 914	1 168	1 593	1 895	1 484	1 093
Turkey	88	215	271	241	304	336	496	559	600	548
UK	8 260	8 189	8 307	9 240	9 881	9 878	9 270	8 859	8 736	7 884
European NATO	**27 235**	**28 293**	**29 543**	**31 554**	**32 137**	**31 659**	**32 207**	**33 672**	**33 342**	**32 413**
NATO total	**68 630**	**74 958**	**82 441**	**92 818**	**100 379**	**106 360**	**112 313**	**115 126**	**107 170**	**106 086**
EC countries	26 735	28 269	28 820	30 762	31 397	30 612	31 166	32 516	32 170	30 984

Sources: NATO publications; authors' calculations. Figures for France are based on national data.

Similar forecasts for the USA show that if the present rates of reductions continue, it will take 12 years, or until 2002, for procurement spending on major weapons to reach the level it had at the beginning of the Reagan Administration buildup in 1980. However, history also shows that rapid procurement buildups in the USA have very quickly been reversed once the process of disarmament speeds up. For example, the Viet Nam War military expansion saw procurement budgets rise from $51 billion to $86 billion (in constant 1989 prices) between FYs 1965 and 1969. Yet, by FY 1973 spending had fallen to $47 billion.

These estimates indicate that political will is central to the control of weapon acquisition. There is no automatic mechanism by which arms control will guarantee reductions. Since technological sophistication is costly, modernization can continue and costs can escalate even with deep cuts in numbers and low ceilings.

As regards individual countries, over the past three years the trends point modestly downwards for the major European NATO countries, that is, the FRG, the UK and (to a lesser extent) France. In addition to overall budgetary constraints and market saturation, recent progress in arms control may have had an impact, particularly for the FRG. However, the downward trend is not firmly established and may change in the absence of political motivation. In addition, procurement cycles could have produced lower expenditures in the latter half of the 1980s, after the rapid rise in the first half of the decade. In Italy procurement spending on major weapons rose steadily throughout the decade and shows no sign of abating.

Another trend worth noting is that for the three major European NATO countries, procurement declines were matched by similar changes in R&D expenditures. For the FRG, the budget category of *Forschung und Entwicklung* (R&D) increased steadily while the value of *Materialbeschaffung* (procurement) fell rapidly (in real terms) from 1986 to 1989. In the UK, real spending on all categories has declined since around FY 1986. However, the fall in R&D expenditure is much less than that in procurement. For France, the proportion of the total defence budget allocated to *Études* (R&D) has grown during the past three years.[17]

---

[17] The data for the UK, the FRG and France are from *Statement of the Defence Estimates, 1989–1990*, vol. 2 (Her Majesty's Stationery Office: London, 1989); *IAP Dienst Sicherheitspolitik*, no. 24/23 (23 Nov. 1989), p. 10; *Erläuterungen und Vergleiche zum Regierungs-*

It is possible that such 'forward-looking' spending on R&D will tend to pull up defence expenditure for these three European NATO countries, which take the lion's share of research activities in the region. As new weapon systems are developed, tested and evaluated, pressure for acquisition will mount in the future. This would point to a future rise in military expenditure, after a lag, unless arms control measures result not only in the destruction of existing assets but also in a slow-down of modernization.

The planning process for reductions in assets in anticipation of a CFE agreement in 1990 began in earnest in 1989.[18] A number of questions remain to be answered: What are the proportions of older and newer weapons to be scrapped? How can the transfer of modern equipment from countries which will have a surplus to countries which can still utilize them be ensured under the agreed-upon counting rules? How can 'rationalization' be achieved so that conventional assets may be distributed among the Allies more equitably? How will the financing of this expensive redistribution take place? Who will pay for what? The problems are complex. As one NATO official acknowledged: 'Look, we have been working for dozens of years to get everyone to standardize their equipment. Now, within six months we are supposed to get everyone to agree on complex technology transfer. It's asking a lot'.[19]

The political transformation in Eastern Europe and the demise of the homogeneous political structure of the WTO mean that NATO's military threat assessment needs to be altered. It has been claimed that conventional war is no longer an option in Europe. Clearly, a purely military alliance is difficult to justify under the circumstances. In 1989 repeated calls were made by President Bush and others in the US Administration to transform NATO into a political bloc. It has also been suggested that it might even have an economic role,[20] presumably to cushion the economic effects of disarmament which may follow from the deep cuts implicit in a future CFE round.

It is anticipated that these changes will have an impact on military expenditure. The most direct consequence of arms control could be the reduction in procurement expenditure and in the cost of major

entwurf des Verteidigungshaushalts 1989 (FRG Ministry of Defence: Bonn, 31 Aug. 1989); and French Ministry of Defence (note 16).

[18] *Washington Times*, 30 Nov. 1989, pp. 1, 21.

[19] Almond, P., 'NATO acts to cut weaponry', *Washington Times*, 1 Nov. 1989, p. 1.

[20] *The Independent*, 16 Oct. 1989.

weapon acquisition, which varies from 15 to 25 per cent of total military spending. The political changes taking place in Eastern Europe will also put pressure on the size and requirements of armed forces in general. It will be difficult to justify large-scale arms programmes that, as now, involve expenditures that add up to 3–4 per cent of the national output, armed forces that make up 2–3 per cent of the labour force and defence spending that amounts to 8–9 per cent of total central government expenditure.

However, the 1989 military expenditure figures for European NATO clearly demonstrate that caution rather than change is the order of the day. According to SIPRI estimates, between 1988 and 1989 there was no decline in military expenditure for the region. Rather there was an overall increase, although it was very modest (on the order of 0.5 per cent) and could have been a statistical artifact. Nevertheless, there is no discernible downward trend over the past few years. The only change is that the growth of defence spending observable in the first half of the 1980s (following NATO's 3 per cent per annum increase directive) has disappeared. Military expenditure is now at a plateau, and political will is needed to bring it down.

3. The EC: community and security

I. Political evolution

The European Community has since its inception been a major player in international economic relations. Its aggregate GDP is catching up with that of the United States, and it has a larger population. The combined military expenditure of all the EC member states is about $150 billion. Compared to two of the largest industrialized countries, this is more than five times of that of Japan but about half of that of the USA, which on the other hand has global interests to maintain. Counting only the US expenditure for European commitments, total EC military expenditure is roughly comparable to that of the USA. EC aggregate military forces exceed those of the USA. In terms of resources and forces, therefore, it is a major political player. Whether it will take up the initiative to focus on a common foreign and defence policy remains to be seen.

Until the traumatic events of 1989, West European political integration within the context of the EC was proceeding slowly. Even the small changes occurred because of structural factors such as economic alliances rather than for political reasons. As the European Parliament itself stated, 'The Community's advanced level of *economic integration,* particularly in its commercial policy, calls for alignment of the foreign policies of the Member States'.[1] In addition, the political and economic aspects of security were increasingly emphasized, but the military aspects were the exclusive domain of NATO. The Solemn Declaration on European Union, signed by the heads of EC governments in Stuttgart in 1983,[2] affirmed the importance of political and economic security.

The binding concept—that defence co-operation lay outside the ambit of the EC—was stipulated in Article 23(b) of the 1958 Treaty of Rome,[3] which stated: 'Any member state may take such measures

[1] European Parliament Directorate-General for Research, Fact Sheets on the *European Parliament and the Activities of the European Community* (Office for Official Publications of the European Communities: Luxembourg, Sep. 1988); emphasis added.
[2] See note 1.
[3] *Treaties Establishing the European Communities, Treaties Amending these Treaties and Documents Concerning the Accession* (Office for Official Publications of the European Communities: Luxembourg, 1989).

as it considers necessary for the protection of the essential interests of its security which are connected with the production of or trade in arms, munitions and war materiel; such measures shall not adversely affect the conditions of competition in the common market . . .'. However, the operating word was 'may' rather than 'must', and the article is not necessarily a permanently binding principle.[4]

The effect of 'Europe 1992', when a fully fledged, common and integrated market will be set up on the continent, marks an important point in the evolution of the EC and has major implications for political integration. The intergovernmental conference which after some difficulties produced the Single European Act, setting up the integrated market for after 1992,[5] explicitly codified European co-operation in the sphere of foreign policy. Even though the Act never called into question the relevance of the Western European Union or the competence of NATO in security matters, its impact will be felt through greater cohesion among the member countries of the EC.

The emphasis on security policy comes in Article 30 of the Treaty of Rome on 'Treaty provisions on European cooperation in the sphere of foreign policy'. The various paragraphs, particularly 4, 5 and 6,[6] demonstrate the importance that the EC places on its new role. Article 30(4) stresses that the 'European Parliament is closely associated with European Political Co-operation'. Article 30(5) emphasizes that the 'external policies of the EC and the policies agreed in European Political Co-operation must be consistent'. However, most important is Article 30(6), which states emphatically that: 'The High Contracting Parties consider that closer co-operation on questions of European security would contribute in an essential way to the development of a European identity in external policy matters. They are ready to co-ordinate their positions more closely on the political and economic aspects of security'.

There is still a long way to go before these concepts can be translated into institutional structures leading to Euro-federalism, particularly in defence policy. Yet, the debate and pace of integration have definitely accelerated. The latter half of the 1980s saw an increasingly confident Europe aspiring to some form of unity. This is a major change from the first half of the decade: budgetary controversies

---

[4] For a perceptive analysis, see Rupp, R., 'Europe 1992', *NATO's Sixteen Nations*, vol. 34, no. 8 (Jan. 1990).
[5] See note 1.
[6] See note 3.

racked the Commission and threatened the fabric of cohesion; and poor economic performance, labeled as 'Euro-sclerosis', threatened to destroy growth potential. The situation is dramatically different now, with more cohesion among leaders, more confidence in the business sector and rapid economic growth. This is therefore the optimum time to grab the opportunity for more political integration, leading on to a common defence policy.

However, not everything will proceed smoothly. The events of 1989 provoked a debate on the 'widening' or 'deepening' of European structures. The Common Market, the possibilities for economic and monetary union, as well as the economic unification of Germany all require a homogeneous EC. On the other hand, the presence of a democratic Eastern Europe, wanting to join the EC, the difficulty of allaying Soviet security fears and the general degree of uncertainty call for a looser institutional structure. In early 1990, President Mitterrand and Chancellor Kohl explicitly stated their desire for political union by the Community, which cannot but influence defence policy in general and military expenditure in particular. If the USA ultimately withdraws from Europe, then of course a further problem of burden-sharing will emerge, even though the threats are much less.

The major reason why the EC, as a fully fledged economic union, will increasingly play a larger role in security affairs is simply because in the new Europe economic factors are expected to play a dominant role. The balancing of military power and the importance of military security in East–West relations will become less crucial in governing European strategic relations, although it will continue to play an important role. The European peace order will never be stable unless and until there is economic prosperity in all parts of the continent, and here the EC must play a crucial role. However reluctant some governments may be to surrender national sovereignty, political integration usually follows full economic integration.

A number of events in 1989 indicated that a greater role for the EC in international political and security affairs is in the making.

1. There was the co-ordination of all Western assistance (including that of the USA) to the newly democratically-oriented East European countries. Noting that the political renaissance of Eastern Europe could only become meaningful if economic regeneration took place, the Group of Seven countries (Canada, France, the FRG, Italy, Japan,

the UK and the USA) in their 1989 annual summit meeting pledged large sums of foreign assistance (including food aid to Poland). For the first time the EC was entrusted with the task of co-ordinating this effort and acting as a bridge between East and West.[7] Although there was no explicit political mandate, the nature of the task implies an acknowledged foreign policy dimension.

2. The Delors Report (named after Jacques Delors, President of the EC Commission) on economic and monetary union was submitted in April 1989.[8] In it some controversial points were raised relating to budgetary policy, with implications for military expenditures in a future West European entity. Also, as a result of the discussions of the Report at the Madrid and Strasbourg EC summit meetings, the question of the status of the 1958 Treaty of Rome was again raised. The Treaty has by many been considered to forever preclude a common stand on foreign policy. The principle has now been accepted that technical impediments such as Treaty revisions cannot stand in the way of political unity, if this is desired by the EC member states themselves.

3. Preparations for the integrated and single European market in 1992 gathered momentum during 1989. In a 1988 report investigating progress towards the internal market, the EC Commission had stated: 'The question of defence procurement will also need to be addressed in the light of both the provisions of the EEC Treaty and the European Cooperation provisions of the Single Act'.[9] To speed up the market integration process, the EC Commission took a more active interest in public procurement, competition policy within the single market and cross-border mergers. The linkages between procurement budgets, policies and purchases will become crucial, specifically for arms manufacturers. Delors claimed in an interview that the arms industry 'is the most immobile—because of national vanities, captive markets, the power of the military, we do not cooperate sufficiently and we waste money'.[10] Some of the long-term issues are discussed below in section III, in the context of procurement spending. An in-depth

---

[7] *International Herald Tribune*, 17 July 1989, p. 2.

[8] *Report of the Committee for the Study of Economic and Monetary Union* (European Committee: Luxembourg, Apr. 1989). For a perceptive analysis on the Report by an academic Committee member, see Thygesen, N., 'The Delors Report and European integration', *International Affairs*, vol. 65, no. 4 (autumn 1989), pp. 637–52.

[9] *Completing the Internal Market* (Commission of the European Communities: Brussels, 17 Nov. 1988).

[10] See the interview with Delors in *Financial Times*, 14 Mar. 1989.

review of the links between arms control and industry is to be found in the *SIPRI Yearbook 1990*.[11]

4. Finally there was the impact of the changes taking place in Eastern Europe. The effect of this process in the West was to open a floodgate of debate on whether there should be a 'widening' or 'deepening' of European structures. The requirements of EC membership were debated with an explicit political overtone, with particular emphasis on the question of whether the EC is to wait for the East to catch up or to move forward with rapid economic and structural change.

All of these events signal changes that may take place in the military expenditure process and budgetary allocation mechanism. A forward-looking analysis needs therefore to consider these implications seriously. Three major factors stand out as important for the EC member states' future total defence spending. All of them are systemic and long-term, but they were also significantly affected by events in 1989.

1. The first systemic factor relates to a common foreign policy for the EC and consequently a defence policy that will affect military expenditure. The effect of the Single European Act and the integrated market after 1992 means that the EC will have a comprehensive common market for goods, services and labour. In the next stage will come a monetary union with free financial flows (capital movements) across countries and the fixing of exchange-rates. As yet, there is no agreement regarding a common or even 'parallel' currency—one of the proposals advocated by the founders of the European Monetary System, Valéry Giscard d'Estaing and Helmut Schmidt. With a monetary union, however, a common currency would necessarily follow. The next stage envisages an economic union with four components: a single market for all goods and services, a competitive trade policy, common policies for social change and regional development, and co-ordination of national budgets with binding rules for budget deficits.

2. The second factor arises out of the demands for the co-ordination of fiscal policy. Although the British Government is totally opposed

---

[11] See Anthony, I., Courades Allebeck, A., Gullikstad, E., Hagmeyer-Gaverus, G. and Wulf, H., 'Arms production', in SIPRI, *SIPRI Yearbook 1990: World Armaments and Disarmament* (Oxford University Press: Oxford, 1990), chapter 8.

('a diversion from the main course of European debate'[12]) it makes economic sense to have a common budgetary policy for the entire EC; it is difficult to envisage a union of market, money and economy without one. If such an integration does occur, it would be hard to imagine that military expenditure could be kept out of the ambit of the future EC. The UK, France and the FRG spend around 10–12 per cent of their central government expenditure on defence. This is a sizeable proportion, and it must be affected if aggregate budgets are controlled by the EC.

3. The third factor relates to EC interests in opening up all public sector procurement to market forces. This relates directly to defence procurement expenditures, whose size and composition would interact with overall public procurement policy.[13] According to SIPRI estimates, the EC countries spent over $32 billion (in 1988 prices) on *major* weapon purchases alone in 1989. Although some weapon imports will inevitably come from the USA, a dominant part of the demand for such arms will be supplied by European firms. (The British Government, for example, spends 80 per cent of its defence procurement budget within the country.) This is potentially a very large market that under competitive conditions could function much more efficiently than it does at present. In addition, there are other types of procurement spending (on food, fuel and construction material) that could amount to another $42 billion. Public expenditure on buying goods for the defence sector within the EC was worth around $75 billion in 1989.

Three of the four proposals for economic union in the Delors Report would affect the arms industries as well. These relate to the single market, open-bid procurement policies and national budgetary co-ordination (the setting of upper limits to arms purchases).

The primary factors affecting arms industries in the EC can be summarized as 'C⁴I': (arms) control, competition, commercialization, concentration and integration. All of these work through and are closely integrated with the member countries' procurement expenditures, particularly those for major weapon acquisition. Arms control negotiations, if successful in achieving deep cuts, will put pressure on

---

[12] See former Chancellor of the Exchequer Nigel Lawson's speech at the Royal Institute of Economic Affairs, 25 Jan. 1989; Thygesen (note 8); *The Economist*, 22 Apr. 1989, pp. 16, 27.

[13] Walker, W. and Gummett, P., 'Britain and the European armaments market', *International Affairs*, vol. 65, no. 3 (summer 1989), pp. 419–42.

governments to reduce procurement budgets. Lower budgets and higher unit costs (of new-generation equipment) will induce governments to encourage competition in the arms industry. In addition, commercial motives will take precedence over narrow national security interests, and defence ministries will ask for 'value for money' rather than whether there is a viable domestic industry or not. Technology and mergers are already concentrating European defence firms in larger units. If there is lower procurement then the movement towards concentration will continue. At the same time, integration in the civilian economy will force defence subsidiaries also to consider themselves as 'European' in the broader sense of the term, independent of ownership.

II. Economic and military indicators

To evaluate the security role of the EC in the future, it is necessary to have information on its economic and military potential since these will influence its common political behaviour. Although a large volume of data is available, it is not usually grouped together to reflect economic and military power. SIPRI has therefore collected a sample of such information, for the years 1988 and 1980, to reflect the change over the decade. These data are presented in tables 3.1 and 3.2, respectively. To facilitate comparison, all financial figures are in 1988 prices and exchange-rates for both sets of data.

Even though the period of the early 1980s was problematic for the EC, by the end of the decade the Community showed great economic strength and military power as a whole. Collectively, it can be compared positively with the USA: its population is greater; its GDP is nearly the same; its armed forces are larger, at lower costs due to conscription; and its defence spending and weapon procurement expenditure are similar, assuming that 50 per cent of US spending is on Europe. The Community now has the economic strength to maintain a defensive military structure and sustain a defence capability adequate to its needs. Whether this will be formalized under a more integrated political union should be the agenda for discussion.

Table 3.1. Comparative economic and military indicators of the European Community countries, the USA and Japan, 1988

Country	GDP (US $b.)	Population (m.)	Per capita GDP (US $)	Per capita real growth rate 1980–87 (%)	Military expenditure (US $m.)	Armed forces (thou.)	Weapon procurement expenditure (US $m.)
FRG	1 202.0	61.2	19 641	*1.7*	35 097	494.3	5 089
France	949.2	55.9	16 989	*1.1*	36 105	466.3	9 496
Italy	828.9	57.4	14 431	*1.9*	20 429	390.0	4 188
UK	807.5	57.1	14 147	*2.5*	34 629	311.7	8 736
Spain	340.1	39.1	8 709	*1.6*	7 171	285.0	1 484
Netherlands	227.5	14.8	15 413	*1.0*	6 729	103.6	1 373
Belgium	152.5	9.9	15 373	*1.3*	4 107	92.4	492
Denmark	107.6	5.1	20 975	*2.5*	2 320	31.6	334
Greece	53.6	10.0	5 355	*0.9*	3 378	208.5	790
Portugal	41.9	10.4	4 048	*1.0*	1 347	75.3	141
Ireland	31.5	3.5	8 898	*0.3*	462	13.0	45
Luxembourg	7.0	0.4	18 919	*. .*	86	0.8	2
EC total	**4 749.3**	**324.7**	**14 628**[a]	**1.7**[a]	**151 860**	**2 472.5**	**32 170**
USA	4 839.4	246.3	19 646	*2.1*	294 901	2 124.9	71 808
Japan	2 858.9	122.6	23 317	*3.2*	28 521	247.0	7 964

[a] Average figure.

Sources: SIPRI data base; authors' calculations.

Table 3.2. Comparative economic and military indicators of the European Community countries, the USA and Japan, 1980

Country	GDP (US $b.)	Population (m.)	Per capita GDP (US $)	Per capita real growth rate 1980–87 (%)	Military expenditure (US $m.)	Armed forces (thou.)	Weapon procurement expenditure (US $m.)
FRG	1 030.5	61.6	16 729	2.6	33 807	495.0	5 003
France	810.3	53.9	15 033	3.0	32 222	494.7	6 863
Italy	669.9	56.4	11 878	2.4	14 174	366.0	2 482
UK	658.3	56.0	11 755	1.8	31 100	329.2	8 260
Spain	278.8	37.5	7 435	3.0	6 423	342.0	1 265
Netherlands	209.2	14.1	14 837	2.1	6 510	115.0	1 178
Belgium	140.2	9.9	14 162	2.8	4 614	87.9	663
Denmark	130.3	5.1	20 255	2.1	2 235	35.1	360
Greece	50.1	9.6	5 219	4.0	2 841	181.5	534
Portugal	33.1	9.8	3 378	3.3	1 145	59.5	70
Ireland	27.9	3.4	8 206	2.4	525	14.8	56
Luxembourg	5.8	0.4	14 500	6.8	60	0.7	1.1
EC total	**4 017.4**	**317.7**	**143 387**[a]	**3.0**[a]	**135 656**	**2 521.4**	**26 735.1**
USA	3 851.4	227.8	15 907	2.7	206 573	2 050.0	40 281
Japan	2 179.4	116.8	18 659	4.6	20 099	241.0	4 174

[a] Average figure.

Sources: SIPRI data base; authors' calculations.

4. Eastern Europe: new beginnings

I. Introduction

Far-reaching economic reforms are now under way in all of Eastern Europe. Central planning is expected to be abandoned, and the command structure of the economy is being replaced by decentralized economic decision making. The most advanced of such market-oriented reforms have taken place in Hungary, which has experimented with a mixed economy for some time. The most rapid transformation is taking place in Poland, where the dismantling of the state economic apparatus is to be completed by the end of 1990.

Grave economic crisis threatens most of these countries, and structural adjustments may cause great hardships in the short term. Having faced the problems of communism—shortages, queues, low-quality products, black markets and systemic corruption—they are about to face the problems of capitalism—unemployment, inflation and inequality. There are few easy solutions. As is the case for the USSR, foreign policy is now intricately linked with the domestic economic process. In the interests of European stability, Eastern Europe must succeed in its economic and political reforms. The specific problems of external debt and economic crisis are dealt with in chapter 9.

In the case of the non-Soviet WTO (NSWTO) countries, two issues deserve particular attention: defence burden-shedding and defence burden-sharing. The first relates directly to events in 1989, when large reductions were claimed. The second relates to the past and future role of Soviet forces in the defence of Eastern Europe as a whole. Analysis of burden-sharing also permits an evaluation of whether the withdrawal of Soviet troops, as required by arms control agreements, in economic terms will mainly benefit Eastern Europe or the USSR.

II. Burden-shedding

Following President Gorbachev's lead and prodded both by economic difficulties and the desire for arms control, in early 1989 almost all the NSWTO countries announced sizeable reductions in defence budgets and armed forces.[1] Bulgaria stated that in 1989 it reduced its military spending by 12 per cent from the level of the previous year. Czechoslovakia claimed a reduction of 15 per cent in 1989–90. The German Democratic Republic announced a cut of 10 per cent in 1989–90 as well. Romania had already claimed that it had made some reductions in 1985–88; no new cuts were announced in 1989.

In the case of Hungary some difficulties remain in the interpretation of the data. New budgetary accounting methods have been introduced, and the time series and the trend may not be comparable with what has previously been published by the Hungarian Government. The Hungarian Parliament refused to ratify the defence budget for 1989, claiming that the proposed cut was insufficient. It is now claimed that total *real* reductions in 1989 will amount to 17 per cent for Hungary. If true, this could be the largest military expenditure reduction in the wave of cuts within the WTO.

In the case of Poland the situation is similar to that of many Latin American countries, in that it is becoming extremely difficult to estimate military expenditure because of high inflation. The original Polish budget for 1989 was almost double that of the level set for 1988. However, inflation in 1988 was more than 50 per cent, and the Government probably expected prices to rise much faster in 1989, probably more than 100 per cent. In other words, there would in any case have been a real reduction. Actual inflation is now claimed to be running at 500 per cent or more, which means that if military expenditure in money terms has not risen fivefold, there has been a cut. Although precise figures for Poland's actual military expenditure in 1989 are not available as yet, it is expected that the real reduction is of the order of 5 per cent.

In addition to cuts in military expenditure, there are reports of force and armament reductions in the WTO countries. For example, in 1989–90 the Polish Army is to reduce the strength of its forces by 40 000 from its current level of over 400 000 men. In addition, 850 tanks, 900 artillery, 700 armoured troop carriers and 80 aircraft are to be removed from the inventory. Similarly, the Hungarian armed forces will be reduced by 9300 men, 250 tanks, 430 artillery and 9 air defence aircraft.

---

[1] See the following 1989 issues of *Jane's Defence Weekly*: 7 Jan., p. 6; 14 Jan., p. 43; 21 Jan., p. 82; 11 Feb., p. 250; 25 Feb., p. 305; 24 June, pp. 1314–15; 7 Oct., p. 719; 4 Nov., p. 973.

Little is known from domestic sources about NSWTO defence spending and allocations. Detailed information has been considered a state secret. A general picture can be obtained from the single-line entries for defence budgets, and from occasional snippets of information as to whether or not border guards or internal security personnel are included. An elementary functional division, between investment and current military expenditures, is provided in the Polish defence budget only, although the investment element is so small that it cannot include procurement. R&D expenditures are generally not revealed, although it is thought that only Poland and Czechoslovakia (the two major arms-producing countries using indigenous designs) have sizeable military research budgets.

The situation is changing fast, however. One of the basic CSBMs is the detailed revelation of military expenditure and its allocation. With greater transparency of military budgets it will be possible to know more about the defence burdens of these countries. In early 1990 the Polish Ministry of Defence published a very informative White Paper, in which it is claimed that the defence burden is of the order of 3 per cent and that military expenditure as a proportion of the state budget declined from 8.5 to 6.3 per cent between 1987 and 1988. The allocation of the 1988 budget with its constituent components is given as follows: personnel, 58 per cent; procurement, 23 per cent; construction, 1 per cent; and operations and maintenance, 18 per cent. It is not known under which category military R&D falls in the Polish budget.

In spite of the paucity of data and the general secrecy surrounding military spending in NSWTO countries, however, there is more confidence in the NSWTO aggregate figure than in the corresponding figure for the USSR. The reason is that, unlike the near-constant Soviet budget, NSWTO military expenditures have risen consistently with their national products. There has been a close connection between military spending trends and general economic trends. Also, known force modernizations have been reflected in the figures for revealed military expenditure. An important study by the US Defense Intelligence Agency using the building-block method, which costs components of the defence sector (military personnel, individual weapons and military R&D) in US prices and dollars, has shown that overall there is little discrepancy between official budget data and the

DIA's own estimates.[2] This is in stark contrast to the DIA analysis for the USSR, which implies that even the new figures presented by President Gorbachev could be only half of their own estimates.

Using the building-block method, the DIA has produced cost figures for Czechoslovakia, Hungary, Poland and Romania which are only 15 per cent higher than the amounts given in the official military expenditure budgets for these countries. For the GDR, the DIA figures are even *lower* than the official data. Until 1989, Bulgaria was the only country in the WTO which had not published any military expenditure data at all for the previous 10 years.

Taken together, the total defence spending of the six NSWTO countries is much less than that of either the UK, the FRG or France.[3] In spite of the low absolute figures for aggregate defence spending, however, the growth rate of military expenditure has been high for the NSWTO countries. The growth rates of defence spending are roughly comparable between NATO and the WTO during the 1980s. In a sense the WTO responded, in classic arms race fashion, to the NATO 3 per cent 'rule'. Between 1980 and 1989, using SIPRI data, it can be shown that the growth of defence spending for the NSWTO countries *taken as a whole* was almost 4 per cent per annum, probably higher than even in the USSR. In 1989, however, the burden began to be reduced in earnest. Military expenditure for the six countries fell by 4.7 per cent in 1988–89, and the downward trend is set to continue.

III. Burden-sharing

As Soviet troops plan to leave Eastern Europe, and member countries such as Hungary are even considering leaving the WTO, the discussion of burden-sharing seems increasingly academic. It is important, however, to analyse how the WTO countries shared the costs of alliance. If the costs to the NSWTO have been high, economic gains

[2] See Clements, T. W., 'The costs of defence in the non-Soviet Warsaw Pact: a historical perspective', *East European Economies: Slow Growth in the 1980s, vol. 1: Economic Performance and Policy, Papers submitted to the Joint Economic Committee* (US Government Printing Office: Washington, DC, 1985), pp. 451–74. See also, in the same volume, Alton, T. P., Lazarcik, G., Bass, E. A. and Badach, K., 'East European defense expenditures 1965–1982', pp. 475–501. For an earlier analysis of burden-sharing see Rice, C., 'Defense burden-sharing', eds D. Holloway and J. M. O. Sharp, *The Warsaw Pact: Alliance in Transition?* (Macmillan: London, 1984).

[3] SIPRI uses a purchasing power parity measure to change local currencies of the NATO countries to US dollars and hence maintains rough comparability of dollar costs with other countries, since the exchange-rates do not reflect world price differentials.

may be made from a future Soviet withdrawal. Alternatively, if the USSR has been shouldering most of the burden, then the cost of ensuring security without a Soviet presence will rise in the long run. As long as Europe is not demilitarized, caution will require that security forces be maintained at relatively high levels. If the NSWTO countries currently are 'free riders', they would have to compensate for future Soviet withdrawals by expanding their own defence commitments and costs.

The main problem with analysing WTO burden-sharing is the lack of reasonable data even at the aggregate level. Military expenditure data in a common currency (generally the US dollar) are difficult to estimate because suitable conversion rates are not easy to find. Official exchange-rates in the past have generally been meaningless since they do not reflect price structures but are officially set. Purchasing power parities are either not available on a time-series basis, or differ substantially between defence and national product, or are unreliable, varying considerably from one analysis to another. Again, the building-block method seems to provide the best estimates. It is widely believed that such estimates are upwardly biased. However, if the bias exists in one direction only, and is relatively uniform, then it should not distort the value of shares and ratios.

Table 4.1 gives military expenditure figures for the WTO countries in two groups (NSWTO and the USSR). It should be emphasized that the data are based on Western intelligence estimates and are not derived by SIPRI. However, SIPRI has made adjustments utilizing its own estimates of real growth rate (to measure volume changes between 1980 and 1988); in addition, the US military price deflator has been used to obtain price changes and current dollar estimates for the two years.

It is clear that the USSR shoulders the lion's share of WTO spending on defence. The NSWTO countries account for about 16 per cent of total WTO expenditure and 25 per cent of the armed forces. Even if its global and strategic commitments are taken into account, the USSR still accounts for the overwhelming share of total expenditures. For example, if it is assumed that only 50 per cent of Soviet military spending is for Europe, then NSWTO spending corresponds to about one-third of total WTO spending. As regards the armed forces, NSWTO troop strengths are about a quarter of the total, that is, the

Table 4.1. Burden-sharing in the Warsaw Treaty Organization, 1980 and 1988

	Military expenditure (US $b.)		Armed forces (thousands)	
	1980	1988	1980	1988
Non-Soviet WTO	32	58	1 345	1 451
USSR	174	303	4 100	4 000
WTO total	**206**	**361**	**5 445**	**5 851**
Non-Soviet WTO share of total (%)	*16*	*16*	*25*	*25*

Sources: Clements, T. W., 'The costs of defence in the non-Soviet Warsaw Pact: a historical perspective', *East European Economies: Slow Growth in the 1980s, vol. 1: Economic Performance and Policy, Papers submitted to the Joint Economic Committee* (US Government Printing Office: Washington, DC, 1985), pp. 451–74; US Arms Control and Disarmament Agency, *World Military Expenditure and Arms Transfers 1988* (ACDA: Washington, DC, 1988); authors' estimates.

ratio of forces maintained between the USSR and the other members of the WTO is approximately 3:1.

From military expenditure figures it is clear that there has been little burden-sharing within the WTO. Most of the costs of collective security have been borne by the USSR during peacetime, probably on the assumption that some advantages will accrue during a conflict.

For the host countries there could have been indirect costs associated with the Soviet bases, such as for construction, operations and support. The basing agreements for the GDR, Hungary and Poland do not specify who pays for what. The Polish Status of Forces Agreement with the Soviet Union states that the forces will utilize barracks, exercise grounds, artillery ranges, buildings, equipment, means of transport, electric power, and public and commercial services and that the rates of pay will be determined in a separate agreement.[4] Since costing is not stipulated, it is not possible to estimate whether the share paid by host governments is high or not. There is

---

[4] Text of the *Treaty on the Legal Status of Soviet Troops Temporarily Stationed in Poland, Warsaw, 17 December 1956, Zbiór Dokumentów* [Collection of Documents] 1956, no. 12 (Polish Institute of International Affairs: Warsaw, 1956), pp. 1879–90. Similar treaties were signed with other WTO countries. For Hungary, for instance, see *Treaty on the Legal Status of Soviet Troops Temporarily Stationed in Hungary, Budapest, 27 May 1957, Zbiór Dokumentów* [Collection of Documents] 1957, no. 5 (Polish Institute of International Affairs: Warsaw, 1957), pp. 1273–85.

more detail in the Czechoslovak Status of Forces Agreement from 1968. A Rand Corporation study analyses it thus:

It stipulates that the Soviet Union will cover maintenance costs, but Czechoslovakia will provide barracks, housing, service, warehouses, airfields, and other services. Soviet trade establishments are to purchase goods and services from their Czech counterpart for sale to Soviet troops at state retail prices minus the wholesale discount. The Soviets pay in transferable rubles converted into koruna at a ratio determined by the ratio of domestic Czech prices to foreign trade prices. *None of this evidence indicates that the East Europeans cover any of the operational costs of the Soviet troops located in their countries.*[5]

The same Rand study also claims that the USSR probably bears most of the variable costs of its troops at the bases: weapons, ammunition and spares are Soviet, since East European manufacture is not standardized; wages are paid in roubles; and subsistence is also paid for as the above-mentioned Czechoslovak Agreement shows. Major weapons almost certainly belong to the USSR. Thus the only expenditure to the host government is probably for the construction and maintenance of the bases. Whether or not the USSR pays rent as well is not known. However, the host countries have probably paid large sums for hidden costs outside the normal defence budget. These would include expenditures for transportation, water, electricity and waste disposal. In addition, the opportunity costs of rents and taxes forgone on prime land and facilities could be substantial. Nothing is known about such costs to the NSWTO countries.

It has also been claimed that the USSR could have forced the NSWTO countries to increase their military expenditure, even if not warranted by changing threat perceptions or economic growth. This would be strong evidence of coercion as well as of indirect costs that would have to be accounted for as a burden. This seems to have been the case at the WTO Political Consultative Committee meeting in 1978. In response to NATO's call for a 3 per cent growth rate of annual military expenditure, the USSR persuaded the WTO to call for a corresponding increase. With one notable exception, however, the NSWTO countries failed to meet this goal. Throughout the 1980s economic constraints played a far greater role in controlling NSWTO defence spending than any Soviet coercion. Only the GDR showed

[5] Crane, K., *Military Spending in Eastern Europe*, Prepared for the Office of the Under Secretary of Defense (Rand Corp.: Santa Monica, Calif., 1987); emphasis added.

large increases in defence spending, which may be explained by the fact that its economy is by far the healthiest in Eastern Europe. The GDR is also the one WTO country in which the USSR is in some way reimbursed for its defence commitments.

Overall, the NSWTO countries have contributed less to alliance security than would have been possible if the USSR had not assumed so much of the common burden. The alliance has been of greater political and military significance to the USSR than to the other allies, and it has also shouldered a greater economic burden. Conversely, the NSWTO countries have probably acted as 'free riders' in an economic sense. However, the requirements of security imposed by the USSR on the WTO were undesirable to the East European countries, and the new governments of Czechoslovakia, Hungary and Poland have already informed Moscow that all Soviet troops must leave and the bases be shut down.[6]

[6] *Financial Times*, 19 Jan. 1990, p. 18.

5. The United States: dollars and deficits

I. Introduction

One of the most remarkable transformations in the evolution of military expenditure during the 1980s took place in the United States. Responding to the alleged 'military expenditure gap' with respect to the Soviet Union, President Reagan rapidly accelerated the arms buildup that had already *modestly* begun under President Carter. According to SIPRI data, US military expenditure rose by almost 50 per cent between 1980 and 1986, or at a rate of 6.7 per cent per annum. This rate of growth far exceeded that of any other industrialized country during this period. More important, from the point of view of qualitative arms dynamics, was the fact that spending on arms procurement and R&D rose faster than the aggregate. For example, spending on major weapon procurement almost doubled during this period, increasing at a rate of 11.6 per cent per annum.

However, Reagan's last year in office saw the emergence of an *entente cordiale* between the superpowers, which would have been unthinkable in the earlier years of his Administration. There was a startling change in the US perception of the USSR, from the concept of the 'evil empire' to the triumphant Moscow summit meeting and the signing of the INF Treaty, considered by many to be a landmark in recent arms control negotiations. Changes in East–West relations and the overall political climate had become even more profound by the time President Bush entered office in 1989. However, the US defence budgets, except in terms of underlying trends, have yet to respond to this euphoria in international relations. Domestic considerations, the state of the economy, the level of the aggregate deficit and the complex web of congressional co-operation and conflict with the Administration are all still as important in determining the size of the defence budget as is the demise of the fundamental conflict in the post-war era.

In terms of military expenditure limitations, much was expected at the beginning of the new presidency, but the response to date has been

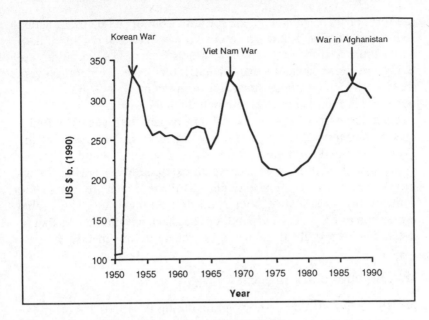

Figure 5.1. US military expenditure, FYs 1950–90

cautious. 1989 was the first year of President George Bush's Administration. It was a year of both continuity and change. Continuity characterized domestic policy, with the President in conflict and co-operation with Congress regarding the budget deficit and its impact on various categories of government expenditure, including defence. Change marked US foreign policy, with the initially cautious President pressed to keep apace with the swift transitions in Eastern Europe and the promise of success in the arms control process.

By FY 1989, in terms of budget outlays, military expenditure had fallen for the second successive year. According to US budget authority, defence spending has fallen for four successive years.[1] The trend for US military expenditure is clearly downward, reinforced by technological, economic and political forces for disarmament, the latter in

---

[1] For details see the following: *Budget of the United States Government 1990* (US Government Printing Office: Washington, DC, 1989); *United States Budget in Brief 1990* (US Government Printing Office: Washington, DC, 1989); *Special Analyses, Budget of the United States Government 1990* (US Government Printing Office: Washington, DC, 1989); *National Defense Budget Estimates for 1989/1990* (Office of the Assistant Secretary of Defense (Comptroller), US Department of Defense: Washington, DC, 1989).

the form of increasing demands for arms control. As of 1989, actual reductions were modest when compared with the rapid rise in military expenditure over the first half of the 1980s. Plans and expectations are being cut more savagely than actual forces or equipment. Nevertheless, given the hopes regarding arms control, US military expenditure is expected to fall more rapidly in the future.

Over the past 41 years, US military expenditure has exhibited a classic long-term cyclical pattern (see figure 5.1). The 'peaks' of the cycle coincided with three wars: two saw active combat by the country, and the third was seen as an example of a growing Soviet global threat. Intriguingly enough, all of these were fought in the Third World—in Korea, Viet Nam and Afghanistan. The global dimension to US defence expenditure has been as important as that of defending the homeland and having European commitments.

II. The budgetary process

As US defence spending grew rapidly during the 1980s and other expenditures were not curtailed equivalently, a central issue was how to finance these increases. The economic model on which Reagan policies were based—so-called 'Reaganomics'—called for lower taxation (to increase incentives and productivity) as well as controlling the money supply (to reduce inflation). The only alternative was to increase heavily government borrowing (bond issue) to finance the budget deficit, since revenue (from taxes, for example) was insufficient to pay for the rising expenditure (mostly propelled by defence and entitlement spending). Owing to the sheer size of the US Government spending, its large-scale borrowing raised national interest rates, which in turn had important international repercussions.

Both contractionary monetary policy and the increase in borrowing raised the money rate of interest while controlling the rate of inflation. Thus the real rate of interest rose rapidly. This caused an inflow of foreign financial capital into the USA, which in turn forced the dollar to rise in value or appreciate very quickly. The 'overshooting' of the dollar (above its long-term sustainable rate) caused US competitiveness to decline and exports to fall. The general boom in the economy, fuelled by rising government spending, at the same time made imports rise quickly. These declining exports and rising imports produced a massive trade deficit, which steadily assumed alarming proportions.

The 'twin deficits'—of budget and trade—emanating from rapidly rising military expenditure created fundamental structural weaknesses in the economy which needed to be tackled.

The Wall Street crash of October 1987 and the concomitant difficulties of the world economy were strong reminders to the Administration that the US Government and nation could not continue to be the largest corporate debtors of the world. The two macroeconomic deficits needed to be tackled in a co-ordinated fashion. In the absence of strong action from the Administration, Congress passed the Gramm–Rudman–Hollings Act[2] on budget deficit reduction which stipulates progressively reduced levels of budget deficit until it is eliminated altogether. This Act imposes progressive targeted reductions in deficits such that a balanced budget is reached in 1992, but it also provides for a margin of error of $10 billion for each year's target. Breaking this ceiling would imply across-the-board cuts, which would destroy the rationale of the basic fiscal structure proposed by the Executive. For FY 1989, running from 1 October 1988 to 30 September 1989, the Act stipulates the aggregate deficit value to be $136 billion. Inclusive of the additional $10 billion (for errors), the target would be $146 billion. Even though the target is sought to be maintained at the start of the fiscal year, through assumptions about the behaviour of the economy in the coming year, there is no penalty for overshooting the level at the end. The actual deficits have therefore exceeded the Gramm–Rudman–Hollings Act targets. In FY 1989, for example, the actual deficit was expected to be above the $146 billion level. There is little hope that by FY 1992 the deficit will be zero, as required by the Act.

The intricacies of US fiscal legislation, which have an important effect on defence spending and force structures, can be understood more clearly by analysing in detail a particular year and seeing how military spending is determined. A detailed analysis for 1989 is presented below.

[2] The first version was called the Balanced Budget and Emergency Deficit Control Act. After being declared unconstitutional, the new version was called the Balanced Budget and Emergency Deficit Reduction Reaffirmation Act. The main difference is that, in the former, expenditure cuts would come into operation on the basis of the economic forecasts by the CBO; the latter stipulates that the relevant forecasts are those by the OMB, a part of the Administration. It should be noted that the OMB forecasts have generally been more optimistic about future trends and have allowed the Government more room to manoeuvre in its expenditure programmes. See *The Economist*, 24–30 Sep. 1988, which also provides a perceptive survey of the US and world economies.

The year began with the traditional bipartisan concord between Congress and the new President. By the summer, however, the consensus seemed to have broken down, as a result of Bush's insistence on reducing capital gains tax—a measure disapproved by the Democratic Party since it tends to favour the wealthier sections of society. In October 1989 the Gramm–Rudman–Hollings Act ceiling on the budget deficit was invoked,[3] since agreement to hold the budget deficit to $110 billion (as estimated by the Office of Management and Budget) failed to materialize. However, a late compromise was reached in November, when the President signed the appropriations measures which established the budget law for FY 1990 (1 October 1989 to 30 September 1990). The result was a mixture of confusion and cuts (some across the board), demonstrating the short-term nature of the annual US budgetary process. Defence spending was also reduced, although by less than what was originally expected. If a compromise had not been reached, the mandatory cuts under the Gramm–Rudman–Hollings Act would have meant a reduction from the original budget authority by $13 billion in US defence spending for FY 1990. This could potentially have been the largest reduction of the 1980s. (Ironically, it would have been the result not of arms control measures, but of the peculiarities of the US fiscal and legislative processes.) In practice, however, the actual reduction from the original budget was much less—of the order of $4 billion.

In addition, long-term prospects of significant arms reductions, emanating from the democratization process in Eastern Europe and positive shifts in Soviet foreign policy, are also putting pressure on the defence budget. There is now need for a formal re-evaluation of US strategic policy, to take account of the combined effect of these short-term and long-term pressures.

The US budgetary process for FY 1990 was more complicated than usual, as the outgoing and the incoming Presidents presented different budgets. Nevertheless, there were similarities in objectives and spending patterns, and the total amount of resources allocated in each budget did not differ greatly. The following discussion concentrates on budget outlays (rather than budget authority), since this corresponds more closely to the amount actually spent.

---

[3] See Deger, S., 'World military expenditure', SIPRI, *SIPRI Yearbook 1989: World Armaments and Disarmament* (Oxford University Press: Oxford, 1989), p. 135, including note 1.

In January 1989 President Reagan presented his FY 1990 budget, in which $303 billion were allocated to national defence. The estimated outlay for FY 1989 was $298.3 billion. The increase of about $4.7 billion was not enough to cover inflation, however, meaning that even in the last Reagan budget there was a real decline. It should be noted in this regard that the budget authority originally requested by Reagan was a 2 per cent real growth (from $298.8 billion in FY 1989 to $315.2 billion in FY 1990).

President Bush's budget for FY 1990 was presented in February 1989. He opted for 'zero growth' in his budget authority. The estimated value of national defence outlay for FY 1990 presented by Bush amounted to about $300.6 billion. This figure was disputed by the Congressional Budget Office, however, which estimated that military programmes would result in an outlay of $304 billion.[4]

In April an initial budget agreement was reached by congressional leaders on a bipartisan level. As mentioned, however, various problems, in particular the controversy about capital gains tax reductions, stopped the agreement from being binding. In October, at the beginning of the budgetary year (FY 1990), the budget had still not been finalized and a sequestration, required by the Gramm–Rudman–Hollings Act, came into effect. The Act's ceiling on the aggregate budget deficit in FY 1990 is $100 billion plus 10 per cent discretionary. The aggregate budget deficit must therefore be less than $110 billion. According to estimates made by the OMB in October 1989 (at the beginning of FY 1990), the Bush budget deficit would significantly exceed this ceiling, hence the sequestration order. Various compromises, and some imaginative accounting practices, allowed the final budget bill to be signed two months after the beginning of the fiscal year. To bring the forecasted budget deficit down to the maximum permitted level, the sequestration order operated until February 1990, but the final effect on the defence budget will probably be a minimal reduction of about $1.7 billion.

It is estimated that the outlay for national defence in FY 1990 will be approximately $300 billion, which is about $2 billion more than the appropriations for the previous fiscal year. Taking into account the inflation rate, there is a real decline of over 3 per cent from FY 1989 to FY 1990, supporting the trend of a modestly falling defence budget. The DOD receives $286 billion, and the rest is allocated to defence-

[4] *Congressional Quarterly*, vol. 47, no. 7 (25 Nov. 1989).

related activities, in particular to the nuclear programmes of the Department of Energy. A new element of the funding structure was the reduction of the SDI budget from its 1989 allocation, the first such reduction in the six years that the programme has existed. In his budget proposal President Bush had requested $4.9 billion, but he settled for $3.8 billion, a cut in proposed funding of $1.1 billion.[5] Significantly, however, the cut meant a reduction in money terms of only $234 million from President Reagan's 1989 SDI budget. This being said, it should also be noted that in the FY 1991 defence budget, presented in January 1990, the funding requested for SDI will allow it to reach a new high of $4.5 billion.[6]

One of the most startling pronouncements regarding US military expenditure in 1989 was made by Secretary of Defense Richard Cheney, who in November stated that there were plans to reduce the DOD budget by $180 billion over five years. This turned out to be much less dramatic than was first thought. What Cheney did was to conduct a hypothetical budget planning exercise. The armed services were asked to calculate the effect of an annual 5 per cent real reduction in their budgets for FYs 1991–94, instead of, as in the current defence plan, a 1 per cent real annual growth in FYs 1991–92 and a 2 per cent real annual growth in FYs 1993–94. Each of the armed services was asked to suggest cuts that would allow the DOD to accommodate the new budget plan. The Army proposed to demobilize 90 000–200 000 men (the equivalent of three active divisions) and to cancel the upgrade programme of the M-1 Abrams main battle tank (called M-1A2) or to cut back estimated annual production from 600 to 200 units. The Air Force proposed to reduce production of F-16 fighter aircraft from 150 to 108 per year, to slow down purchase of the B-2 bomber, to close 15 bases and to cut five fighter wings. The Navy proposed to reduce the number of carrier groups from the planned 14 to 12, to cut personnel by 10 per cent (60 000 men), and to scrap 62 ships and settle for a 500-ship Navy.[7]

These plans may be interpreted in two ways. From the military's point of view, the cuts are real. The anticipated levels of forces and assets from which the reductions are to be made were based on security needs established by the Government. Lower levels of pro-

[5] *Washington Times*, 30 Nov. 1989, p. 6.

[6] *The Guardian*, 29 Jan. 1990; *The Guardian*, 30 Jan. 1990.

[7] *Defense News*, vol. 4, no. 48 (27 Nov. 1989), p.1; *The Economist*, 25 Nov. 1989, p. 47; *Business Week*, 4 Dec. 1989, p. 32.

jected military assets are therefore a significant indication of reduced defence capability. However, from a financial point of view, the new plans are less significant since the cuts are taking place from an unrealistically projected budget baseline. In a 'zero growth scenario' many of these cuts would take place automatically, since the total defence budget allocation would be insufficient. If future arms control agreements require deep cuts, then the spending plans from which the hypothesized cuts have been estimated become even less relevant.

III. The past

During the decade of the 1980s the USA spent over $2300 billion on military expenditure. Out of this total, about $635 billion was spent on personnel costs (27.6 per cent), about $609 billion on weapon procurement (26.5 per cent) and $255 billion on R&D (11.1 per cent). Table 5.1 gives the detailed allocations.

Table 5.1. US national defence expenditure outlays, FYs 1980–89

Figures are in US $b., current prices.

	1980	1981	1982	1983	1984	1985	1986	1987	1988	1989
Personnel	40.9	47.9	55.2	60.9	64.2	67.8	71.5	72.0	76.3	78.2
O&M	44.8	51.9	59.7	64.9	67.4	72.4	75.3	76.2	84.5	85.4
Procurement	29.0	35.2	43.3	53.6	61.9	70.4	76.5	80.7	77.2	80.7
RDT&E	13.1	15.3	17.7	20.6	23.1	27.1	32.3	33.6	34.8	37.0
Energy, defence	2.9	3.4	4.3	5.2	6.1	7.1	7.4	7.5	7.9	7.9
Other	3.3	3.8	5.1	4.7	4.7	7.9	10.4	12	9.7	9.1
Total	**134.0**	**157.5**	**185.3**	**209.9**	**227.4**	**252.7**	**273.4**	**282.0**	**290.4**	**298.3**

Source: *United States Budget in Brief* (US Government Printing Office: Washington, DC, 1989).

In the 40 years from FY 1951 to FY 1990, US DOD outlays peaked three times: they reached $260.5 billion in FY 1953, in part due to the Korean War effort; $293.6 billion in FY 1968, the highest in the Viet Nam War period; and $296.4 billion (in constant FY 1989 prices) in FY 1987. As the figures show, the highest annual DOD expenditure over the past four decades was recorded at the end of the Reagan Administration.

This massive expenditure was used to attain the largest peacetime buildup ever of the US military. In addition to the quantitative expansion, there was also a massive investment in qualitative improvements. This includes technological innovations (such as 'stealth' technology), increasing R&D systems enhancement (such as systems for destroying deeply buried or mobile targets) and rapid modernization (two new bomber forces, the B-1B and the B-2, within the same decade). It would be surprising if this amount of funding did not buy much in terms of new technology. However, a cost–benefit analysis should also consider whether this expansion and modernization resulted in substantial improvements in force structure, capabilities and efficiency.[8]

As regards the armed forces, there was little proportional change in active duty military personnel between FY 1980 and FY 1989, with a growth of less than 1 per cent per year. Only the Navy increased its personnel figures substantially. The Army added two light divisions, probably suited for low-intensity conflict and rapid deployment.

Modernization continued throughout the decade, but the number of new major weapons could for reasons of cost not match the vast increase in procurement and R&D expenditure. For new weapons, unit costs increase with annual production rates; only after a large cumulative total production (a threshold) do unit costs start declining. For example, the decision to reduce purchases of MX missiles from 100 to 50 will raise unit costs, although total spending on the package will be less than planned. (If the Midgetman Small ICBM is added on to the arsenal to compensate for the reduction in MX missiles—as Congress did in 1989 by funding both—then total costs will not be less.) To take another example, although the B-2 bomber is equipped with exotic 'stealth' technology that, according to its proponents, 'threatens to render Soviet air defences obsolete' and to undermine totally the Soviet Air Defence system,[9] the $70 billion price tag for the whole package (possibly rising to $100 billion, or one-third of the annual

---

[8] Niskanen, W. A., 'More defense spending for smaller forces: what hath the DOD wrought', *Policy Analysis* (CATO Institute), no. 110 (29 July 1988), pp. 1–21.

[9] The quote is taken from Lepingwell, J. W. R., 'Soviet strategic air defense and the Stealth challenge', *International Security*, vol. 14, no. 2 (autumn 1989), p. 64. There are currently 5 air programmes which embody 'stealth' technology: the Advanced Cruise Missile (ACM), the Advanced Technology Bomber (ATB) or B-2, the Air Force's Advanced Tactical Fighter (ATF), the Navy's Advanced Tactical Aircraft and the F-117A. For a general review of 'stealth' technology, see Welch, J., 'Assessing the value of stealthy aircraft and cruise missiles', *International Security*, vol. 14, no. 2 (autumn 1989), pp. 47–63.

defence budget, if operations and support costs are included) is clearly too steep to be accepted without challenge. Congress has allowed two planes to be bought in FY 1990 and has begun a searching critique of the system's usefulness. As Senator William Cohen wrote in 1989: 'The B-2 bomber: mission questionable, cost impossible'.[10]

Survivability of ICBMs in response to a first strike has been a key indicator of the efficiency of the strategic nuclear triad.[11] The debate continued during 1989, as it had done over the decade, with few results. According to plans, the MX missiles, currently based in hardened silos, are to be dispersed over seven states and placed on railcars. Congress appropriated $1.1 billion in FY 1990 for their redeployment. The total cost, including operations and support, will be $12 billion for the 50 in stock, with each armed with 10 multiple independently targetable re-entry vehicles (MIRVs). The argument over vulnerability has gone through so many twists and turns, however, that continued silo basing may be preferred. Congress also authorized $1.1 billion for FY 1990 to make the single-MIRV Midgetman road mobile.[12] However, the issue of survivability, and hence efficiency, remains debatable.

As regards force readiness and sustainability, little seems to have changed. According to the DOD, 'mission capable' equipment was only 'slightly increasing' or may have remained constant during 1980–85.[13] Only in terms of the quality of military personnel can the US military claim unequivocal success during this period. Qualification and experience have increased, as has the ability to handle complex weapon systems, yet personnel expenditure has grown the least in comparison with procurement, O&M, and R&D; thus combat efficiency has increased at minimum cost.

The allocation of such massive levels of military expenditure throughout the decade (see table 5.2 for yearly figures) will also have an indirect influence. This can be explained in terms of 'push' and 'pull' factors. The 'push' effect works when budget authority rises

---

[10] Cohen, W. S., 'The B-2 bomber: mission questionable, cost impossible', *Arms Control Today*, vol. 19, no. 8 (Oct. 1988), pp. 3–8.

[11] For a general discussion, see Carnesale, A., 'The enduring problem of ICBM basing', ed. E. H. Arnett, *US Strategic Forces Modernization Under Arms Control and Budget Constraints*, proceedings from a seminar for members of Congress and congressional staff, 1 June 1989 (American Association for the Advancement of Science: Washington, DC, 1989).

[12] *New York Times*, 30 Nov. 1989, p 1.

[13] See Niskanen (note 8).

Table 5.2. US national defence expenditure authority, FYs 1980–89

Figures are percentages.

	1980	1981	1982	1983	1984	1985	1986	1987	1988	1989
Personnel	33.0	30.1	27.7	26.3	25.5	23.3	23.5	26.0	26.5	26.7
O&M	30.4	29.3	27.9	27.0	27.1	27.1	27.0	28.8	29.2	29.8
Procurement	24.4	27.2	30.6	33.8	33.4	33.8	32.8	28.6	28.1	27.2
RDT&E	9.3	9.3	9.5	9.6	10.4	10.8	12.0	12.8	12.9	13.0
Other	2.9	4.1	4.3	3.3	3.6	5	4.7	3.8	3.3	3.3

Source: SIPRI data base.

faster (or falls more slowly) than budget outlay or actual spending. As the investment component (procurement, construction and R&D) of the US military budget grew rapidly compared to operating costs (personnel and O&M), the 'push' factor became important. In effect, funding is authorized for a single year, but spending takes place over a longer period for weapon research, development, testing, evaluation (RDT&E) and purchase. If expenditure has to be reduced for such obligations, inherited from the past, then cancellations (with extra penalty costs) are required. However, cancellations create political problems, and the Government is unwilling to upset major defence contractors. Expenditures on such practically automatic obligations take up about 40 per cent of the spending budget.[14] Total pay (and pensions) consume another 40 per cent. Therefore, 80 per cent of annual military spending cannot be touched in the medium term; it is as if 80 per cent of the budget is already committed even before the fiscal year begins.

The 'pull' factor operates when RDT&E expenditure rises fast, particularly for sophisticated technology, such as that used in the 'stealth' or SDI Phase I programmes. When projects are near completion they tend to 'pull up' expenditures. Proponents can claim that it would be 'wasteful' not to continue procurement. For example, it was argued in 1989 that the $23 billion already invested in the B-2 programme (until recently classified information) would be wasted if the programme were to be cancelled at this stage. As RDT&E spending was the fastest-growing outlay of the US defence budget in the 1980s, as shown in table 5.1, it is clear that this 'pull' factor will remain significant in the 1990s.

[14] Adams, G. and Cain, S. A., 'Defense dilemmas in the 1990s', *International Security*, vol. 13, no. 4 (spring 1989), pp. 5–15.

The trend of military expenditure in the medium term may change as the military seeks to achieve a balance between essentially political factors (arms control and negotiations) and techno-economic factors (unwarranted technological sophistication and subsequent cost increases). Representative Dennis Hertel, of the House Armed Services Committee, said in 1989: 'If the top chain of command decided a plane must be able to fly faster than the speed of light, travel backwards in time to attack targets throughout history, and complete the mission by landing on the sun, the acquisition system may express greater reservation about the scientific problem than about the cost or necessity of doing any of these things'.[15] This state of affairs could definitely change in what may be termed a 'scissors crisis', with the two blades of the scissors, one political and the other structural, forcing the relevant cuts.

The very scale of defence-related spending has increased concern over Pentagon waste, inefficiency, industrial fraud and graft, which remain major issues. The year 1988, for example, saw a large-scale action by the US Federal Bureau of Investigation to uncover evidence after two years of investigations. Some predictions are dramatic: a source claimed that such corruption could trigger 'legislative intervention and moving the industry substantially closer to effective nationalization'.[16] In 1988 the Senate and the House passed stringent regulations to overcome the obvious gaps in the system, but the scale of corruption is often related to the level of procurement; in spite of some cuts the total budget is still high, and its spending could continue to support illegal practices.

US military capability today is far greater than it was at the beginning of the current Administration. It is debatable whether its military strength was the dominant factor in bringing about the *rapprochement* with the USSR, which allegedly was forced to a negotiating position from a position of relative weakness. It is also

---

[15] Rep. Dennis M. Hertel, House Armed Services Committee, in a statement from 16 Aug. 1989, quoted in *Defence Monitor*, vol. 18, no. 7 (1989), p. 2.

[16] *Defense News*, vol. 3, no. 25 (20 June 1988), p. 1. An audit by the DOD revealed that between July 1984 and Sep. 1987 industrial suppliers had overcharged the Pentagon by $789 million; *Financial Times*, 10 Aug. 1988. The scale of corruption has also led to more self-regulatory controls in the fear that the Government may intervene more actively than it has hitherto done. On the self-regulation of Pentagon industrial contractors, see *Defense News*, vol. 3, no. 30 (1988), p. 4. The President's Commission on Defense Management, known as the Packard Commission after its Chairman, David Packard, has suggested the setting up of a Defense Industry Initiative on Business Ethics and Conduct which will be the core of self-regulatory practices to discourage corruption.

controversial as to whether there has been value for the money; even a purely strategic cost–benefit analysis could reveal that things could have been managed more efficiently. Some critical gaps remain:[17] transport ships and planes to carry troops abroad in pursuance of international security interests are inadequate; shortages in ammunition stockpiles still create problems; and the debate, in the context of the strategic nuclear force, about the choice of missiles and how to protect them (in silos or with rail-basing) still continues. However, overall, there can be little doubt that purely in terms of war-fighting capability and deterrence the strategy has been successful. In particular, personnel numbers, training and morale are high, partly motivated by better training and pay.

None the less, no country, however rich and powerful, can view its military expenditure process independent of the other myriad domestic and international factors that constitute the security environment, defined in the broadest sense. From a purely historical point of view, all great nations have had to balance investment, welfare and defence if they were to maintain their pre-eminent position and prevent over-stretching their economic limits. The USA is no different. The historian Paul Kennedy, in his book *The Rise and Fall of the Great Powers*,[18] makes this clear and has already created a stir with his prediction that the USA could be reaching that limit because of its high defence spending.

However, caution should be exercised in reaching quick conclusions about the postulated negative impact. US security spending has been dominated by long cycles. Between 1969 and 1979 it fell in real terms by 34.6 per cent. In the past 10 years (1979–89) it rose by 51.9 per cent. The difference is dramatic. The burden of military spending is not necessarily heavy because of the relative size of the defence sector compared to the country's resources. After all, the USA is an economic giant. During World War II it spent over 35 per cent of its GNP on defence and yet emerged as the economically most powerful nation on earth. Even during the 1950s, a period of prosperity and growth, it regularly spent 10–14 per cent of its national income on the military. The crucial point is the rapidity with which such a massive peacetime military buildup has been accomplished. This is what has created the many economic problems. Correspondingly, a reduction, if

---

[17] *International Herald Tribune*, 13 Dec. 1988.
[18] Kennedy, P., *The Rise and Fall of the Great Powers: Economic Change and Military Conflict from 1500 to 2000* (Random House: New York, 1987).

Table 5.3. US budget and trade deficits, 1980–89

Figures are in US $b.

Year	Budget deficit[a]	Trade balance[b]
1980	72.7	+ 1.9
1981	73.9	+ 6.9
1982	120.0	– 7.0
1983	208.0	– 44.3
1984	185.6	– 104.2
1985	221.6	– 112.7
1986	237.9	– 133.3
1987	169.3	– 143.7
1988	193.9	– 126.5
1989	217.5	– 106.0

[a] Budgets are for fiscal years.

[b] Trade figures are for calendar years. (+) indicates a surplus, and (–) indicates a deficit.

Sources: *The United States Budget in Brief Fiscal Year 1990* (US Government Printing Office: Washington, DC, 1989); and International Monetary Fund, *World Economic Outlook,* May 1990 and Oct. 1988.

possible, could be equally troublesome if it is made too fast and too soon. Unfortunately, the economics of arms control could be as problematic as that of re-armament.

The key to the dilemma lies in the twin deficits: government budget and foreign trade. Table 5.3 gives the data for the years 1980–89. As discussed above, by cutting taxes and controlling monetary growth, the increase in spending and the resultant budget deficit were financed by public borrowing. This raised US interest rates and made the dollar more attractive to investors world-wide.[19] The consequent increase in the value of the dollar led to exports becoming more expensive and importers cheaper. The result was the trade deficit. In addition, large-scale fiscal spending created a boom in the economy directly, as old-fashioned Keynesian economics has said it would for a long time. But

[19] For a theoretical and policy analysis of the impact of the overvaluation of the dollar, see Dornbusch, R., *Dollars, Debts and Deficits* (MIT Press: Cambridge, Mass., 1986). Professor Dornbusch's ideas follow mainstream open-economy macro-economics, and this is a brief summary of the concepts. A more radical version of the implications of the twin deficits, although following from the 19th century British economist David Ricardo, is that by Professor Robert Barro. He argues that the two deficits are not related; hence cutting the budget will not necessarily improve the trade balance. For a general summary of his work, see Barro, R., 'The Ricardian Approach to Budget Deficits', NBER working paper 2685; a non-technical review appeared in *The Economist*, 10 Dec. 1988.

what happens if this process is reversed quickly? A decline in government spending will reduce the need to borrow. Interest rates will fall, making the dollar weak; but the depreciation of the dollar will also make US imports more expensive. In other words, other countries will not be able to sell to one of the largest market sin the world. Countries such as the UK or France, Third World newly industrializing countries (such as South Korea), and debtors will find it difficult to export and grow as fast as before or to service their past debt. It is generally accepted that if the dollar falls too rapidly, a 'hard landing', then world-wide economic prosperity may suffer badly. The solution to the present situation may be as difficult to handle as the original problem.

Finally, the social impact of the Reagan era should not be forgotten. The priority structure (or welfare function) of this government has been radically different from its predecessors. It has been estimated that defence expenditure will be $270 billion more than it would have been if pre-Reagan budgetary trends had been maintained; similarly, social security and compulsory entitlement spending (owing to unemployment, poverty, medicare, etc.) will be $360 billion more; and non-military and non-entitlements (such as for roads or infrastructure) will be $300 billion less.[20] The implications are clear: the Reagan years have contributed to an unprecedented peacetime military buildup, increased the number and deprivation of people at the lower levels of society who now need more minimal benefits from the Government,[21] and dramatically reduced state involvement in the economic infrastructure.

[20] These estimates are by John Makin of the American Enterprise Institute; see *International Herald Tribune*, 20–21 Feb. 1988.

[21] A wide-ranging review of the social and economic impact of the entire Reagan Administration can be found in Rothschild, E., 'The real Reagan economy', *New York Review*, 31 June 1988; and 'The Reagan economic legacy', *New York Review*, 21 July 1988. In particular, the contrast between booming employment creation and rising social deprivation is emphasized. It seems surprising that, when entitlement expenditures are high, it is also a reflection of poverty and inequality in US society. This is because the Government is constitutionally obliged to provide minimum entitlement relief; when this is high, the implication is that there are more poor people who have to be provided a very minimum standard of living (through income supplements) and health facilities. Sivard, R. L., *World Military and Social Expenditure 1987–88* (World Priorities: Washington, DC, 1987) provides strong evidence on the adverse social impact of the Reagan Administration policies: in 1987 the demand for emergency shelter and food rose by 20%; the minimum wage has dropped in real terms since 1981 so that by 1987 a full-time job at the minimum wage gives an annual income which was $2000 less than the poverty line for a family of three; welfare benefits in

IV. The future

There are three factors that will shape the future of US military expenditure. First, there is the speed of arms control. Even more than the actual levels negotiated, the very fact that the CFE Negotiation and the CSCE are taking place puts political pressure on the Administration to reduce defence spending. Second, the improving political climate in Europe and the remarkable domestic transformation in East European countries imply that threat perceptions need to be modified. The spectre of WTO military spending can no longer be used to justify increases in US defence expenditure. Third, technological and economic structural disarmament will cause cancellations or postponement of major programmes. The future may therefore see not only an end to military spending growth but, more important, a reduction of US strategic commitments.

As regards cost savings arising from arms control negotiations, the current benefits are expected to be small. Estimates produced by the Congressional Budget Office (CBO), based on NATO reduction proposals in mid-1989, show that the savings accruing to the US Government will be of the order of $3 billion, or about 1 per cent of the aggregate budget—an insignificant sum.[22] The latest troop proposal cuts to a ceiling of 195 000, outlined in Bush's State of the Union Message in January 1990, will mean further reductions over and above those calculated in the CBO study. However, preliminary estimates show that even this will mean an overall reduction of 2 per cent per year, no different from what happened in any case during the late 1980s. Much more important is the changing perception of threat and the fact that the WTO has ceased to be an effective alliance capable of fighting together in any orderly fashion. It will also be difficult to explain to voters at home why deep cuts are not taking

1987, for mothers and children in poverty, were 11% less in real value compared with the level 10 years earlier. There is also the related question as to whether it was these entitlement expenditures (and other non-military spending) which caused the budget deficit to rise rather than the defence budget expansion and the cut in taxes. The former view has been echoed by the White House as well as in the Bush election campaign, but this is not substantiated by the facts. As a percentage of GNP, revenues in FY amount to 19%; if the Reagan-era *increases* in interest payment (owing to the expanding national debt) and defence spending are removed, then total expenditure would amount to almost the same percentage of GNP. The *additional* spending, over and above the *trend*, on these two items, defence and interest, is almost exactly equal to the aggregate deficit. Estimated *net* interest payment in FY 1989 exceeded the established budget deficit; see also *International Herald Tribune*, 11 Oct. 1988.

[22] US Congress, Congressional Budget Office, *Budget and Military Effects of a Treaty Limiting Conventional Forces in Europe* (CBO: Washington, DC, Jan. 1990).

place when reality seems to have overtaken political will so completely. Finally, cost increases and the ultra-sophistication of technology also mean that the Government may simply not be able to 'afford' certain types of weapon system. Cost increases for new weapon programmes have reached dizzying heights. The aggregate price index (deflator) of military systems incorporates a factor for technological progress; hence, it does not properly reflect the astronomical price rises of individual weapon systems because they are attributed to higher quality or effectiveness. Yet, procurement budgets will have to allocate resources for these qualitative improvements; and, if allocations do not rise in commensurate fashion, then the number of weapons will have to be reduced or cancelled altogether. The classic case is that of the B-2 bomber. The development of 'stealth' or low-observable (LO) technology incorporated in the aircraft has been conducted in great secrecy, comparable to the Manhattan project which produced the first atomic bomb. The capability of LO technology is immense. Claims are made that it can delude any practical and known air defence system. However, the costs are correspondingly high. Based on an initial order of 132 aircraft, the purchase price comes to over $500 million each. If the orders are reduced, as Cheney indicated in early 1990, then the cost rises to over $800 million each. If further cuts are made in the total number purchased, or alternatively, if all other support, maintenance and additional weapon costs are included, the B-2 becomes the first billion-dollar aeroplane in history. As a means of comparison, the total US Air Force procurement budget in 1989 was of the order of $16 billion. Thus 16–32 B-2s (depending on the price) could exhaust the entire annual budget for all air equipment purchases. It is difficult to see how the economic and technological aspects of US arms purchases can be squared.

The Bush Administration has inherited a costly legacy of military commitments. These include the construction of a space-based 'shield' to protect military targets against a nuclear attack, the ability to deter potential aggressors with strategic nuclear forces as well as substantial conventional forces, to defend Europe and provide stability in a period of rapid change, to protect bases around the globe, to conduct low-intensity warfare anywhere in the Third World, to control the high seas, to provide substantial security assistance to a large number of countries and to project power in defence of US as well as allied interests anywhere.

In 1989 a number of specific concerns surfaced in all these areas. These include discussions on the modernization of the Lance short-range missile; the possible withdrawal of some US forces from Europe and the role of the USA within the changing political and military structure of Europe; a congressional amendment to the defence bill asking for greater Japanese burden-sharing; military assistance to Colombia for narcotics control; the use of US air facilities in the Philippines to help Philippine President Corazon Aquino put down a military revolt; and the invasion of Panama.

One of the most innovative and detailed proposals for deep cuts in forces, assets and US military expenditure has recently come from Professor William Kaufmann. He has advocated proposals which could in principle almost halve defence spending: from the current $300 billion to $160 billion (in constant prices) within this decade. He claims:

Cumulatively, the United States could save more than $500 billion [during the 1990s] if the military competition were replaced by a cooperative reduction of armaments. Now that the Soviet leadership has recognized how much it has suffered from the competition, and how high the cost as proved, an opportunity presents itself to put an end to the military contest and to the risks that accompany it.[23]

The plan assumes that, for the interests of stability and moderately worst-case scenarios that defence planners need to postulate, radical changes cannot come in the short run and in one stage alone. The changes are therefore relatively conservative and hence in principle more acceptable to the defence establishment. The reductions in budgets and forces will need to be phased over three stages and over 10 years.

The first stage, covering 1990–94, envisages negative real growth of military budgets by about 3.1 per cent per annum. In other words, defence spending will decline (after inflationary adjustments are taken into account), from the 1990 level of around $300 billion to $265 billion. The main thrust will be in cuts of strategic nuclear forces, keeping SDI at the research stage only, postponement of some new generation of costly conventional weapons as well as a reduction of naval carrier battle groups from the current 14 to 12 in number.

[23] Kaufmann, W. W., 'A plan to cut military spending in half', *Bulletin of the Atomic Scientists*, Mar. 1990, pp. 35–39.

The second stage, overlapping with the first, will continue until 1996 or 1997. This will be characterized by the implementation of treaties such as the START and CFE agreements. The budgetary implications are modest; however, the political significance is high since it will demonstrate the willingness of former adversaries to formalize arms control in verifiable treaties. The costs for national defence will fall, under the postulated measures, to around $251 billion.

The third stage, which will begin in around 1997 or 1998 and can proceed until the year 2000, will be the most dramatic. It envisages reductions from $251 billion at the end of stage two to a level of around $160 billion per year—lower than at any period since the 1950s. If successful it will mean truly the end of the cold war and the way of thinking that is associated with it.

In this context, it would seem to be important for the President to order a defence review to chart the course of military expenditure for the 1990s.[24] Technology and economics are bound to push for structural disarmament. It is now necessary to utilize the political incentives for arms control to negotiate a substantive deal and then re-order domestic priorities. SIPRI estimates show that, with a 4 per cent per annum real reduction in US military expenditure over the five fiscal years 1990–94, the US DOD budget would still be higher (after adjustment is made for inflation) than in any peacetime period in the history of the United States prior to FY 1983. The impact would in fact be greater than if the Cheney cuts were implemented, since the latter, as discussed above, are based on unrealistically high baselines. In other words, a major and substantial real reduction would still leave US military expenditure at historically unprecedented levels for peacetime operations. SIPRI estimates also show that if US defence spending were to be reduced by 8 per cent annually (after adjusting for inflation) over FYs 1990–94, it would still leave US military expenditure in 1994 at the level inherited by the Reagan Administration. It will not be easy to reverse the arms dynamics as seen through the military expenditure process.

[24] Kaufmann, W. W., 'Restructuring defense', *Brookings Review*, vol. 7, no. 1 (winter 1988–89), pp. 63–67, analyses the conflicting pressures and the hard choices that the President has to face. See also the more general analysis in the context of US foreign policy: Steinbrunner, J. D., *Restructuring American Foreign Policy* (Brookings Institution: Washington, DC, 1989).

6. The Soviet Union: *glasnost* and *perestroika*

I. Introduction

For the Soviet Union 1989 was an important year, with the coming together of three movements, each marked by both successes and failures: the opening of the political system, a more determined effort towards economic restructuring and the attempts to demilitarize foreign policy. All three relate to the issue of military expenditure. The new openness in the political system made possible the publication of credible Soviet defence spending figures. Economic changes have required the re-allocation of resources from the defence sector. The reduction of military expenditure and force levels has reduced threat perceptions and allowed foreign policy to be less militarized.

In spite of significant foreign policy successes, the crucial constraint of the reforms instituted under President Gorbachev seems to be domestic economic and political problems. There is now a close link between achievements on the home front (particularly the availability of food and consumer goods), the continuation of the present leadership's political programmes and the conduct of foreign policy, specifically in the area of arms control. As Academician Vitali Zhurkin rightly points out: 'The problem of carefully *coordinating foreign policy and domestic goals* and the methods for achieving them become all the more important'.[1]

There are numerous aspects of Soviet military expenditure that are currently of interest. The financial figures cannot be properly evaluated, nor their implications understood, unless they are related to a number of wide-ranging factors, both military and economic. The discussion on Soviet military spending is related to budgetary allocations, procurement targets, economic reforms, industrial organization and foreign policy objectives. To impose some order in the discussion, the subsequent analysis is conducted under the headings of

---

[1] Zhurkin, V., Karagonov, S. and Kortunov, A., 'New and old challenges to security', *Kommunist*, no. 1 (1988), p. 42. For an evaluation, see also Gross, N., 'Glasnost and the Soviet military', *RUSI and Brassey's Defence Yearbook 1989* (Brassey's: London, 1989), pp. 159–73; emphasis added.

glasnost, perestroika and *konversiya*. Under the rubric of *glasnost*, the implications of all available information are discussed. The section on *perestroika* analyses the nature of restructuring in the military sector and the possibilities for significant reductions in defence spending. The framework of *konversiya* used here is much broader than the usual concept of industrial conversion; it encompasses resource re-allocation and investigates whether the defence sector can provide the panacea for the problems that the overall Gorbachev reform programme now faces.

II. *Glasnost*: what is known?

After many years of presenting an increasingly untenable figure, the Soviet Government, consistent with the spirit of *glasnost* and confidence-building measures, in 1989 presented a figure (in roubles) for military spending that has a semblance of reality. The reason for not revealing the truth earlier was given by General Mikhail Moiseyev, Chief of the General Staff of the Soviet Armed Forces:

Knowledge of the defence budget allows many people to judge . . . a country's defence capability . . . For this reason many countries of the world sought to conceal the part of their budget allocated for defence . . . Taking into consideration the military and political situation in the world and guided by the need to accelerate the solution of the difficult and numerous problems involved in the building of socialism, the Soviet state had to conceal information about its defence expenditures and changes in this process.[2]

On 30 May 1989, President Gorbachev, speaking to the Congress of People's Deputies, announced that the Soviet military expenditure for the current year would be 77.3 billion roubles—a figure almost four times higher than the official defence budget of 20.2 billion roubles. He said:

But in the modern world the possibilities are increasing for security to be safeguarded by political and diplomatic means. This enables military spending to be cut on the basis of giving a new quality to the USSR Armed Forces without any detriment to the country's defence capability. In 1987–1988 military spending was frozen; this made a savings in the budget, in comparison of the 5-year plan, of R10 billion. Here I am announcing to the Congress this real figure for military spending: R77.3 billion. There is a

[2] Moiseyev, M. (Gen.), 'Soviet defence budget', *Pravda*, 11 June 1989.

proposal being made to reduce military spending as early as 1990–1991 by another R10 billion, that is by 14 percent . . .[3]

These figures are somewhat lower than the SIPRI estimates produced in December 1988 and published in the *SIPRI Yearbook 1989*, placing Soviet defence spending in the neighbourhood of 80 billion roubles plus 10–20 per cent for unaccountable elements.[4]

In news media presentations of the new official figures, Western intelligence estimates in the range of around 120 billion roubles were also cited.[5] A recent NATO estimate puts the 1987 defence outlay of the USSR at between 130 and 140 billion roubles.[6] Prime Minister Margaret Thatcher is reported to have claimed in Parliament that the stated amount was only half of that which Western experts believe to be the actual Soviet expenditure.[7] The DOD claims, in its publication *Soviet Military Power 1989*, that the Soviet Union spent $150 billion on its military in 1988.[8] A perceptive Soviet economist has cast doubt on the absolute spending figure as well as on the figure for the military burden (military spending as a proportion of GNP). He claims that both figures, and in particular that for the defence burden, are too low relative to what is known about Soviet military capability and assets.[9] It has also been claimed that some Soviet analysts believe informally that the military burden is of the order of 22–30 per cent of GNP rather than, as is officially stated, 9 per cent.[10] The controversy continues.

More significant than this aggregate are the allocations of the total amount to personnel, O&M, pensions, procurement, construction and R&D. Table 6.1 shows the figures for 1989 announced by Prime Minister Nikolai Ryzkhov to the Congress of People's Deputies in June. The previously stated spending of 20.2 billion roubles for 1989

[3] From President Gorbachev's speech to the USSR Congress of the People's Deputies on 30 May 1989, published in *Foreign Broadcast Information Service Daily Report: Soviet Union, Supplement; USSR Congress of the People's Deputies* (FBIS-SOV-89-103S), 31 May 1989.
[4] See Deger, S., 'World military expenditure', in SIPRI, *SIPRI Yearbook 1989: World Armaments and Disarmament* (Oxford University Press: Oxford, 1989), pp. 133–94.
[5] Peel, Q., 'Gorbachev reveals "real" defence bill', *Financial Times*, 31 May 1989, p. 3.
[6] Wilkinson, C., 'Soviet defence expenditure: past trends and prospects', *NATO Review*, no. 2 (Apr. 1989), pp. 16–22.
[7] See *Jane's NATO & Europe Today*, vol. 4, no. 38 (13 June 1989), p. 4.
[8] *Soviet Military Power 1989* (US Department of Defense: Washington, DC, 1989).
[9] Izyumov, A., 'Military *glasnost* lacks openness', *Moscow News*, 17–24 Sep. 1989.
[10] Åslund, A., *Gorbachev's Struggle for Economic Reform, 1985–88* (Pinter: London, 1989).

Table 6.1. Official Soviet military expenditure, 1989–90

Figures are in b. current roubles.

	1989	Share (%)	1990	Share (%)	Percentage change 1989–90[a]	Change needed in 1990–91 to meet targets (%)[a, b]
Personnel, O&M	20.2	26.1	19.3	27.3	−4.5	−7.9
Pensions	2.3	3.0	2.4	3.4	+4.4	
Procurement	32.6	42.2	31.0	43.7	−4.9	−11.5
Construction	4.6	6.0	3.7	5.2	−19.6	
R&D	15.3	19.8	13.2	18.6	−13.7	
Others	2.3	3.0	1.3	1.8	−43.5	
Total[c]	77.3	100	71	100	−8.2	−6.6
Military space[d]	3.9					

[a] (−) reduction; (+) increase.
[b] SIPRI estimates.
[c] Items may not add up to totals due to rounding.
[d] For allocations under military space, see page 65.

Sources: *Pravda*, 8 June 1989, p. 3; *Foreign Broadcast Information Service Daily Report: Soviet Union, Supplement; USSR Congress of the People's Deputies* (FBIS-SOV-89-109), 8 June 1989; *Izvestia*, 16 Dec. 1989; authors' estimates.

is now known to cover only personnel costs (salaries and payments to conscripts) and O&M (food, clothing, fuel and repairs). This is only a quarter of the total figures. Major weapon acquisition takes over 40 per cent of spending, and R&D accounts for 20 per cent.

The categories under which the aggregate Soviet figures are divided are similar to the ones used by the United States. In a detailed discussion of the 1989 spending figures General Moiseyev has compared the Soviet figures with those of the USA.[11] In addition to explaining why the figures for the USSR are allegedly low, his analysis also clearly demonstrates the similarities of the various budgetary categories. It also allows independent analysts to check on the plausibility of the figures. In contrast to the Soviet figure, NATO's analysis of the same subject shows a somewhat different picture. Table 6.2 gives the NATO data on the Soviet Union for 1987 (which are not radically different from 1989 data except for a modest inflationary adjustment). The aggregate figures and those for sectorial allocations are vastly different. What is remarkable, however, is the similarity between NATO

[11] Moiseyev, M. (Gen.), 'Soviet defence budget', *Pravda*, 11 June 1989.

Table 6.2. NATO estimates of Soviet military expenditure, 1987

Figures are in b. current roubles.

Item	Low estimate	Percentage share	High estimate	Percentage share
Personnel (incl. pensions)	10.4	*8*	11.2	*8*
O&M	39.0	*30*	42.0	*30*
Procurement	52.0	*40*	56.0	*40*
Construction	2.6	*2*	2.8	*2*
R&D	26.0	*20*	28.0	*20*
Total	**130**	*100*	**140**	*100*

Sources: Wilkinson, C., 'Soviet defence expenditure: past trends and prospects', *NATO Review*, no. 2 (Apr. 1989), pp. 16–22.

and Soviet figures for the cost of procurement (of major weapons) and of R&D as shares of total costs. By all accounts the USSR spends 40 per cent of its total military budget on weapon procurement and 20 per cent on research. Independent of the actual figures, these two shares seem to be exceedingly high. The comparable share for US spending on procurement and research is 27 per cent and 12 per cent (for FY 1989), respectively. The high payments made to volunteer soldiers in the USA tend to make its personnel cost share high and other shares relatively low. But even for the FRG, which has a conscript army, the corresponding proportions are around 21.5 per cent and 6.7 per cent. In a shortage economy, where skills, materials, intermediate inputs, and so on, are insufficient to meet demands, such a large proportionate diversion towards the military simply compounds the already high costs of defence expenditures.[12]

The total military expenditure figures revealed by the Government seem to be of the correct order of magnitude, except for some possible omissions and underestimates. It is not clear, for example, whether the separately announced spending for military space programmes is included in the total budget or not. Expenditure on defence-related space is claimed to be 3.9 billion roubles, out of a total Government outlay on space programmes of 6.9 billion roubles. No separate figures were given for nuclear weapon acquisition by the Soviet strategic forces. In the USA this is funded through the DOE and is not part of

[12] The FRG figures are from *Erläuterungen und Vergleiche zum Regierungsentwurf des Verteidigungshaushalts 1989* (FRG Ministry of Defence: Bonn, 31 Aug. 1989); the US figures are calculated from table 5.1.

the DOD budget, even though it is a component of 'national defence expenditure'. If the USSR follows the same pattern, it is possible that the total of 77.3 billion roubles does not contain spending on this category of weapons. Using the same percentage as in the USA, and making other adjustments, the (possible) exclusion might have reduced the total spending figure by about 10 per cent. There is also no mention of Soviet military aid, which is substantial. Even though the military support to the Afghanistan Government is less burdensome since the troop withdrawal, and the direct cost of stationing forces is eliminated, military assistance still continues. Some estimates have put military aid to Afghanistan at $3 billion per year,[13] but this figure seems to be too high. Nevertheless, military assistance to Afghanistan, Angola, Cambodia and Nicaragua must mean a heavy drain on defence-related spending.

Another category of spending that seems to be relatively low is O&M. The Soviet armed forces are spread over a large geographical area, maintain high-cost foreign bases in Eastern Europe, have a substantial commitment in all four force groupings (land, air, naval and strategic forces) and are required to spend heavily in maintaining a numerically massive inventory of assets. Under the circumstances it is difficult to believe that personnel and maintenance could only be 20.2 billion roubles, about a quarter of total spending. Even accounting for the low costs of conscript pay (although other costs such as food, housing and clothing are similar for officers and conscripts), this category of expenditure needs to be supplemented to arrive at a more reasonable figure.

The main difficulty with assessing Soviet defence expenditure is the arbitrary method by which prices are determined. This is particularly true for major weapons, where the aggregate budget for procurement can be heavily distorted if inappropriate prices are used for costing. The entire Soviet economic system is prone to such problems, since most prices are determined not by market forces but by administrative orders. Hence, when demand exceeds supply there may be 'repressed inflation' and prices may not be able to rise to clear the market. This distortion is increased considerably in priority sectors such as the military industries, where the value of weapons may be fixed independently of cost or demand.

---

[13] See Krauthammar, C., 'Soviet empire: a paradoxical collapse', *International Herald Tribune*, 14–15 Oct. 1989.

General Moiseyev, at a joint press conference with US Admiral William J. Crowe, Jr,[14] claimed that a modern Soviet fighter such as the Su-25 costs 5.8 million roubles. The price of a comparable US F-16 is $28 million. Comparing at an official exchange-rate is meaningless as the Soviet rate is set at artificial levels. Using a purchasing power parity (conversion rate to ensure comparability) of $2.5 to a rouble, the Su-25 would cost $14.5 million, slightly more than half the cost of the F-16. Unless the US production method is terribly inefficient, which is unlikely, there must be an explanation for why in comparable prices its fighter costs twice as much as the Soviet aircraft. One explanation is 'goldplating' (unnecessary expenditure), corruption, cost-plus contracts and high profit rates that are prevalent in the US defence industry. This alone cannot explain the difference, however. An alternative explanation is that the Soviet fighter is underpriced.

It is believed that weapon prices are kept artificially low to accommodate unrealistic budgets. If so, then procurement expenditure on weapon systems is undervalued. In a free market, or even in a planned economy where the military sector is given the same economic priority as the civilian economy, prices and spending on weapons and procurement would be higher than announced. The pricing mechanism of the defence activities has been explained as follows:

Military representatives at each defense plant monitor production and inspect for quality. These representatives also negotiate each year with plant management to reset the established price of the product . . . In the negotiations, the plant manager would argue for keeping the price constant, or more likely, raising it to cover increasing costs. The military representative would counter that the price should be lowered as the plant learns to produce the product more efficiently. The actual price set in a year is determined by the relative bargaining strengths of the two sides . . . Unlike the civilian case, the *price of a military product can be forced down*.[15]

Another controversial problem is how to calculate the share of national product spent on the military. The military burden is difficult to estimate, not only because of the dispute about defence spending

[14] Press conference with General Moiseyev and Admiral Crowe, *Krasnaya Zvezda*, 22 June 1989, p. 3.
[15] US Central Intelligence Agency, *A Guide to Monetary Measures of Soviet Defense Activities, A Reference Aid* (CIA: Washington, DC, Nov. 1987); emphasis added.

but also, more importantly, because of the lack of consensus as to what is the true value of Soviet GNP.[16] There is now a major debate both inside and outside the country regarding the validity of figures on Soviet output and its value. If the GNP is overestimated as claimed, then clearly the military burden will rise even though the estimate of military expenditure remains the same. Official statistics only started giving GNP figures from 1987 onwards; prior to that only net material product (GNP minus most service income) data were provided. Using official data alone the military share in national output is about 8–9 per cent in 1989. This seems to be unrealistically low, given the rough parity that the USSR has with the USA in military capability. Claims at the other extreme give figures as high as 22–30 per cent for the share of the GNP going to the military.

Preliminary SIPRI estimates indicate that Soviet military spending is higher than the Soviet Union has itself claimed but that the orders of magnitude are not fundamentally incorrect. The current SIPRI estimate for Soviet military expenditure for 1988 is 90–100 billion roubles. *Using official GNP figures*, the military burden is estimated by SIPRI to be around 12 per cent, or roughly double that of the USA.[17] If the actual GNP is sizeably lower, the estimate of the military burden will rise commensurably. For example, if Soviet national income is one-third less than its postulated official value, the military burden is 18 per cent, according to the SIPRI estimate.

---

[16] US Central Intelligence Agency, *Revising Soviet Economic Performance Under Glasnost: Implications for CIA Estimates* (CIA: Washington, DC, Sep. 1988).

[17] In 1988 the official Soviet GNP was 866 billion roubles; see *Pravda*, 22 Jan. 1989, p. 3. The NMP was 625 billion roubles, or approximately 72% of GNP; for the NMP figure, see *Izvestia*, 21 Jan. 1989, p. 1. In 1987, the first year in which such data were revealed, the official estimate was 825 billion roubles; see *SSSR v tsifrakh v 1987 godu* [USSR in figures 1987] (Finansy i Statistika: Moscow, 1988). The same source also stated that growth of GNP in 1981–87 was 3.9% per year. This is substantially higher than the widely used CIA data for Soviet national accounts. A critique of various statistical measures is to be found in *Revising Soviet Economic Performance Under Glasnost: Implications for CIA Estimates* (note 16). The UN Economic Commission for Europe, *Economic Survey of Europe in 1988–1989* (United Nations: New York, 1989) also provides an incisive criticism of Soviet statistics, particularly its handling of inflation and growth rates. A major Soviet critic of official claims of high growth rates from the 1960s to the 1980s is Gorbachev's economic adviser, Abel Aganbegîan, who in his book *The Economic Challenge to Perestroika* (Indiana University Press: Bloomington, Ind., 1988) claims that the Soviet growth rate was almost zero in 1981–85. According to official figures, the national income had risen by 16.5% during this period. SIPRI estimates, based on Aganbegîan's figures, show that the actual Soviet GNP figure could be about 33–40% less than the officially stated figure. This has some startling implications. For instance, the figure of 100 billion roubles for military expenditure could imply a defence burden (military expenditure share of national output) of either 12%, using the official GNP figures, or 18–20%, using the alternative estimates of GNP.

It should be stressed that SIPRI relies on open sources only, above all on a wide range of Western sources, the possible bias of which cannot be discounted. Furthermore, these Western sources are surrounded by varying degrees of secrecy as well, meaning that details on methodology and method are often not revealed. For example, it has been claimed by a distinguished sovietologist that the DIA figure for Soviet military spending is derived by simply dividing the total budget by three.[18] Clearly, all independent evaluation is of necessity subjective and subject to margins of error. However, in the absence of more detailed information by either side, there can be no substitute for independent analytical judgements. The usual caveat applies: all statistics in this research area, independent of source, should be treated with extreme care and caution.

III. *Perestroika*: what can be changed?

Of more interest, in terms of international security and threat perception, is whether there are significant reductions in military expenditure currently in the USSR. Almost all sources agree that there are positive signs and that in 1989 Soviet defence spending has been reduced. There are a number of indicators which point in this direction (see table 6.3).

1. The unilateral reductions in armed forces and assets (including 500 000 men, of which one-third are officers) announced at the end of 1988 are being carried out,[19] contributing to a sizeable fall in some categories of spending (although pension and welfare costs may rise somewhat).

2. The 1987 INF Treaty called for the destruction of missiles the maintenance, replacement and modernization of which required moderate amounts of spending.

---

[18] Holzman, F. D., 'Politics and guesswork: CIA and DIA estimates of Soviet military spending', *International Security*, vol. 14, no. 2 (autumn 1989), pp. 101–31, is a devastating critique of the whole estimation procedure used by Western intelligence analysts to calculate Soviet defence spending. For earlier analyses by the same author see, 'Are the Russians really outspending the US on defence?', *International Security*, vol. 4, no. 4 (spring 1980), pp. 86–104; and 'Soviet military spending: assessing the numbers game', *International Security*, vol. 6, no. 4 (spring 1982), pp. 78–101.

[19] On 15 Dec. it was announced that 265 000 troops have been discharged as part of the unilateral reductions; in addition 173 000 troops have been released from conscription. The Soviet Army total for 1 Jan. 1990 has been set at 3 993 000. *Izvestia*, 16 Dec. 1989, TASS report, 15 Dec. 1989; translation in FBIS-SOV-89-103S (note 3).

Table 6.3. Soviet military expenditure reductions, 1989

Area of reduction	Budget category	Expenditure reduction	Comment
Withdrawal from Afghanistan	Personnel O&M	Max. R 5 b. per annum	Military assistance to Afghanistan continues
INF Treaty cuts	O&M Procurement	R 300–500 m. per annum	Costs of elimination of missile systems
Unilateral force reductions	Personnel O&M	R 2.4 b. per annum	Possible dissatisfaction among demobilized forces
Strategic weapon system reductions	Procurement	..	Reduced deployment of SS-18, SS-24, Typhoon, Blackjack
Increased home-porting of naval forces	O&M	..	Possibly linked to demands for naval arms control
New aircraft-carrier cancelled	Procurement	Planned cost of 1 carrier	Linked to naval arms control
3 major plants converted to civilian production	Procurement	Profits to defence ministries	Defence ministries do not bear costs of conversion
Space R&D used for civilian purposes	R&D	..	Overall R&D cuts are not significant for 1989

3. The war in Afghanistan was a financial drain and is reputed to have cost the country 45 billion roubles over eight years. Disinvolvement could save 5 billion roubles per year, although continued military assistance to the Najibullah regime will reduce savings.

4. Civilian industrial activities have begun to replace military production. Thus, defence-related spending will fall as the growth of arms procurement and production is reduced.

5. Recent Western intelligence reports indicate that production and deployments of certain categories of advanced weapons have been halted and such changes must contribute to expenditure cuts.

As mentioned above, according to official information total Soviet defence spending will be reduced during the two years 1990–91 by 14.2 per cent, while procurement cuts will amount to 19.5 per cent. Troop reductions of the order of 12 per cent will also be implemented. In 1991 the planned aggregate Soviet military expenditure is to be 67.3 billion roubles, a reduction of 10 billion roubles from the current level. There is some confusion regarding the time period over which the procurement budget is to be reduced. In a report in *Pravda* in June 1989, General Moiseyev seemed to imply that procurement budget reductions are to take place over the three-year period 1989–91, rather than the two-year period envisaged in President Gorbachev's May announcements.[20] If this is so then reductions in procurement spending were already under way in 1989. That is also consistent with the qualitative information available (see table 6.3). Some reports suggest that in 1989 procurement expenditure was reduced by about 4.5 per cent compared to the 1988 level. It has also been claimed, although in somewhat vague terms, that total reductions from the *planned levels* of military expenditure during the 12th five-year plan 1986–90 are of the order of 30 billion roubles, or 40 per cent of annual defence spending.[21] If this figure is correct it would indeed be a substantial cut. However, as in the case of the Cheney cuts in the US defence budget discussed above, it is difficult to substantiate this figure and to examine its implications.

During November and December 1989, the US news media revealed details of a classified intelligence report (prepared by the DOD, the CIA and the National Security Agency and presented to the President in May) which claimed that the USSR had indeed started the process of reducing its defence spending. It stated that 'there is broad agreement within the US intelligence community' that the USSR 'has decided to reverse a 20 year pattern of growth in military spending and force structure in order to boost the civil economy and Soviet foreign policy'.[22] It also stated that the share of military expenditure in

[20] *Pravda*, 11 June 1989.
[21] Deputy Defence Minister of Armaments General Anatoly Shabanov claims that the projected cuts will save 30 billion roubles; *Jane's Defence Weekly*, vol. 12, no. 16 (21 Oct. 1989), p. 870. In his speech to the Congress of People's Deputies on 7 June, Prime Minister Nikolai Ryzkhov is more explicit: 'Including the proposed reduction of expenditure for the forthcoming 2 years, the overall savings of defense expenses in relation to the approved 5-year plan will amount to nearly R30 billion'; published in FBIS-SOV-89-109S, 8 June 1989, pp. 27–28.
[22] Smith, R. J., 'Soviets slow strategic weapons programs', *Washington Post*, 12 Nov. 1989, p. 1; Friedman, T. L., 'Military spending by Soviets slows', *New York Times*, 14 Nov.

GNP could have fallen from the previously claimed range of 15–17 per cent to 14–16 per cent. These changes in information must have taken place very recently; as late as April 1989, in the annual joint CIA/DIA report to Congress, the claim was made that the postulated defence burden was around 15–17 per cent.[23] Such a change in the share, however, although apparently small (on the order of 1 per cent), implies a dramatic reduction in the level of defence spending. SIPRI estimates, based on such figures, show that military spending itself could have fallen by 6–7 per cent. Supporting these financial figures is information on Soviet procurement and deployment reductions of major strategic weapon systems, such as the Blackjack bomber, the Typhoon Class submarine, and the SS-20 and SS-23 missiles.

It is significant that little qualitative or quantitative information was made available throughout the year on reductions in military R&D activities. Marshal Sergey Akhromeyev, in an interview in *Krasnaya Zvezda*, simply stated: 'A general reduction of military expenditure also means reduction of expenditure for military R&D'.[24]

In his speech detailing defence spending for 1989, Prime Minister Ryzkhov was rather defensive about research expenditure for space programmes. About 57 per cent of all space R&D is on the military; if part of the Buran space shuttle system has military uses then the share rises towards 70 per cent. It is claimed that such technology increases the efficiency of the armed forces by a factor of 1.5–2.[25]

In other statements Soviet military experts have expressed concern about US technological progress in military fields such as 'stealth' technology, anti-satellite capability and space research for SDI. Defence Minister Dmitri Yazov said in September 1989 that: 'As long as a military threat exists the principle of reasonable sufficiency should be backed up by further technological modernization of the

1989, p. 14; Smith, R. J. and Tyler, P. E., 'Bush knew in May of Soviet arms shift', *International Herald Tribune*, 12 Dec. 1989, p. 12.

[23] Central Intelligence Agency/Defense Intelligence Agency, 'The Soviet economy in 1988: Gorbachev changes course', Report presented to the Subcommittee on National Security Economics of the Joint Economic Committee of the US Congress, 14 Apr. 1989 (unpublished mimeo). See also *Allocations of Resources in the Soviet Union and China— 1987*, Hearings before the Subcommittee on National Security Economics of the Joint Economic Committee of the US Congress, 101st Congress (US Government Printing Office: Washington, DC, 1989).

[24] Interview with Marshal S. Akhromeyev in *Krasnaya Zvezda*, 10 May 1989.

[25] Ryzkhov, N., in FBIS-SOV-89-109S, 8 June 1989, pp. 27–28.

armed forces on a qualitatively new basis. And this requires appropriate expenditures'.[26]

Hence, in spite of the reductions in total expenditure and assets, technological modernization and further high R&D could not be ruled out. In November 1989 it was believed that aggregate military expenditure reductions were taking place (although by a relatively small amount in 1989), procurement spending was going down more rapidly than the total budget itself, and R&D was yet to be substantially affected. In December 1989, Soviet military expenditure allocation estimates were published for 1990.[27] It was possible for the first time ever to compare and contrast two successive years of defence allocations as well as to apply consistency checks for discrepancies between earlier plans and current estimates.

The 1990 budget presents a number of surprises (see table 6.1, column 3). Total expenditure is to be reduced by 8.2 per cent; this is consistent with the postulated 14.2 per cent reduction claimed for the two-year period 1990–91. Pensions increase marginally, since demobilized soldiers presumably need extra funding for job losses. However, both procurement expenditures and personnel costs (including O&M) fall by very small amounts. Given the postulated cut of 19.5 per cent for major weapon systems, the actual planned reduction in 1989–90 is only 4.9 per cent. In similar fashion, personnel costs are cut by only 4.5 per cent even though over half of the unilateral troop reductions (500 000 men or 12 per cent of the total) are claimed to have been completed. The greatest surprise is the massive proportionate reduction in R&D expenditures, which are expected to fall by 13.7 per cent. As discussed above, non-financial or qualitative information on technological progress would indicate that research on modernization has not suffered to the same extent as have other parts of the defence sector.

---

[26] The quotation is from an interview with Yazov in *Izvestia*, 16 Sep. 1989. Soviet worries about technological competition with the USA and its ability to keep up with R&D are well known. In particular, SDI has been a perennial headache. In his testimony to the House Armed Services Committee of the US Congress on 21 July 1989, Marshal Akhromeyev suggested that the USA and the USSR should consider a formal agreement to limit military R&D; see *Defense News*, vol. 4, no. 30 (24 July 1989), p. 1. In a rather curt comment in an interview published in *Krasnaya Zvezda*, 10 May 1989, he said that a general reduction of military expenditure means a reduction also of expenditure for military R&D; however, he did not give any figures. Little quantitative information on cuts in research spending in the military sector was available prior to the publication of the 1990 Soviet budget in late 1989.

[27] *Pravda*, 16 Dec. 1989.

In the absence of more details, only informed forecasts can be made. In 1989, the first tentative steps were taken to slow down weapon acquisition and to reduce inventories. In 1990, the slow-down will continue at the same pace. If the target of 19.5 reduction is to be met, the cut in the procurement budget will have to be very large in 1991—of the order of 11.5 per cent. By comparison, in spite of recent talk of US defence cuts, the US DOD has yet to cut its procurement expenditure by more than 5–6 per cent in any one year starting from the mid-1980s. Unless arms control negotiations are formally completed, and the CFE agreement is ratified, it will be difficult to convince the military of such drastic cuts in procurement in one year. Whether the postulated 19.5 per cent reductions in procurement expenditure are to be achieved by the end of 1991 remains to be seen.

In addition, the implied 12 per cent cut in personnel expenditure (due to 12 per cent troop reductions and the fall in associated costs) will require a 7.9 per cent cut in 1991 alone. This is also a very large reduction. SIPRI has made independent estimates from available information about the probable reductions required in 1991 to reach the various announced targets (see table 6.1, column 6). In addition, to meet the targets for 1991, the reductions in personnel and procurement alone (1.5 and 3.5 billion roubles, respectively) will have to be greater than the aggregate budget reduction (4.7 billion roubles). This may mean that some other categories of expenditure, possibly R&D, will rise again.

Many questions remain about the changes in military expenditure and allocation in the Soviet Union. It would be of great help to analysts to receive details about the military expenditure budget for 1988 (and for earlier years as well) so that a real comparison can be made with the facts presented in the 1989 and 1990 budgets. Furthermore, since Prime Minister Ryzkhov has claimed that military expenditure reductions, implemented and continuing until 1991, will save 30 billion roubles from the original five-year plan (1986–90),[28] it should be possible for the authorities to reveal precisely what those earlier planned figures were.

[28] Ryzkhov (note 25).

IV. *Konversiya*: what resources can be re-allocated?

For many years, the Soviet military sector has absorbed vast quantities of resources. High defence spending is an easily identifiable metric or measure that represents the scale of resource diversion, indicative of a wide complex of heterogeneous resources that are suitable for re-allocation. The need now, as President Gorbachev himself has stated, is to transform the 'economy of armament into an economy of disarmament'. 1989 was the first year in which significant attempts were made to redirect resources from the military to the civilian sectors. The question, therefore, is how large and significant this 'disarmament dividend' potentially is.

There are at least 10 ways in which military expenditure reductions and resource re-allocation can help rejuvenate the economy. Even though there are interconnections between them, conceptually they should be kept separate. Furthermore, the cuts will differently affect the various parts of the defence budget—personnel, procurement, construction and R&D.

1. There is the direct impact on the state budget deficit which, in the light of recent revelations, is known to be alarmingly high. In 1989–90 the budget deficit is to be reduced from 120 billion roubles to 60 billion roubles. This is a huge reduction—50 per cent—and it is not very likely that the target will be met. Defence spending cuts are postulated to be about 7 billion roubles. In other words, the military sector will account for just over 11 per cent of the aggregate deficit reduction. Although significant, the contribution is not large.

2. This expenditure could possibly be transferred to other, more useful avenues of social expenditure, such as health or housing. Some expenditure diversion to socio-economic categories has been postulated. For example, it has been suggested that funds (and personnel) from military construction could be used to provide increasingly scarce civilian housing. The largest proportionate cuts in 1989–90 in the military budget have been in construction. The 900 million roubles saved (see table 6.1) could be used to build an estimated 90 000 flats. Government expenditure on health and education must also be a strong priority.[29] It is not surprising that Ryzkhov emphasized health

[29] Fesbach, M., 'Demographic trends in the Soviet Union: serious implications for the Soviet military', *NATO Review*, vol. 37, no. 5 (Oct. 1989), pp. 11–15. The author discusses both general problems associated with health care and its relation to demographic changes

care when he talked about 'the reorientation of the national economy to meet social demands'; in calling for a greater contribution of defence to the national economy he wished that 'above all, this [would apply] to medical equipment'.[30]

3. There is the release of skilled manpower. This is an issue in particular for the Russian and Baltic Republics, faced with demographic changes that will lead to labour shortages. Troop reductions could alleviate such shortages, mainly as regards the need for young and skilled workers. The armed forces constitute 4 per cent of the total labour force, an extremely high figure in a fully employed economy with no additional manpower reserves to draw upon. As a means of comparison, in the USA military personnel as a proportion of the total labour force is around 2.5 per cent; the mainly conscript army of the FRG employs (both civilian and military personnel) about 2.4 per cent of the total labour force. More significantly for the USSR, around 10 per cent of all male Slavs at the university level are conscripted or diverted to the military officer corps.[31] This deprives the economy of its most talented young personnel.

4. There are anticipated future savings to be made as weapons are destroyed under the framework of arms control and O&M costs (particularly for fuel) are slashed. Fixed ceilings on military assets, as implied by the CFE Negotiation, will also mean less replacement of old equipment and the release of physical resources which would otherwise have remained geared to arms production. The INF Treaty apparently created a saving of around 300 million roubles, used to fund the construction of over 30 000 flats.[32] Deep cuts under a CFE agreement will increase such savings in the long run and could provide welcome respite, particularly in what is termed the 'social sphere'.

5. There is the direct contribution that defence factories can make in the provision of machinery for the consumer goods and processed foodstuffs industries, whose output is in short supply and a major source of discontent. Throughout 1988 and 1989 the defence industry ministries and industries were exhorted to increase production and supply of machineries for the food-processing sector. As discussed

which may affect the military. In certain areas of the Soviet Union the infant mortality rate is worse than that of the poorest Third World countries; in Turkmenia, for example, the rate is 51%, which is higher than China, Albania or Mongolia.

[30] Ryzkhov (note 25).
[31] Wilkinson (note 6), p. 20.
[32] Deger (note 4), p. 174, note 46.

above, supply shortages in food and consumer goods could be the main stumbling-block in the short term of the whole reform process, hence the urgency. Five of the nine defence industry ministries[33]— Aviation, Defence, General Machine-Building, Radio Industry and Shipbuilding—have specifically been asked to provide equipment for a variety of food-processing areas, from fruit and vegetable processing to refrigeration equipment to ovens for bakeries. It is planned that these ministries are to provide almost 50 per cent of all machinery required for food processing during 1988–95; the amount of machines expected to come from the military production industries alone is almost equal to the *total* aggregate value of installed machinery in the food-processing sector during this decade.[34]

6. The heavy industrial components of the defence industrial base can be helpful in retooling civilian industries in general and can form the springboard of industrial modernization. Except for the ministries of the Communications, Electronics, Civil Aviation and Radio defence industries, the industry ministries attached to defence production are already involved in the supply of machine tools for the civilian economy. Given the ageing structure of Soviet industries and the heavy investment orientation (high capital output ratios), retooling is clearly essential for technological efficiency. The modest success, or possibly failure, of the earlier quality control programme (*gospriyemka*) in civilian industries has forced the leadership to turn to the military for help.

The machine-building and metal-working (MBMW) sector has planned 'radical measures' to increase its productivity as the main provider of intermediate inputs into the production of consumer goods. Traditionally, the military base has been a mainstay of this sector and will therefore have to take a leading role in this process. Using CIA data, it can be estimated that military procurement constitutes over 50 per cent of MBMW output.[35] With procurement expenditure reduced, part of this output can now be directed to civilian use.

---

[33] There are 9 defence industry ministries: Defence, Aviation, General Machine-Building, Radio, Electronics, Shipbuilding, Communications, Civil Aviation and the State Committee for Computing and Information. For detail, see Cooper, J., 'The defence industry and the new Soviet Government', unpublished mimeo, Centre for Russian and East European Studies (CREES), Birmingham, Aug. 1989. See also the the interview with the Chairman of the Military Industrial Commission, I. S. Belousov, in *Krasnaya Zvezda*, 23 July 1989, p. 2.

[34] See note 23.

[35] Authors' estimate for the late 1980s, based on CIA/DIA (note 23).

7. Some of the current output of the defence factories, particularly in transportation (trucks and helicopters), can be transferred immediately to the civilian sectors. There is now a plethora of information available about such transfers.[36]

8. The product mix of factories producing both civilian and military goods can be transformed in favour of the former. In terms of actual output produced directly, the share of civilian output from the arms-producing industries is to rise from its current level of over 40 per cent to 50 per cent in 1991 and 60 per cent by the middle of the next decade. By the end of the 13th five-year plan, therefore, the Soviet defence industrial base, currently the largest in the world, will be more oriented towards non-military production.[37]

As announced in President Gorbachev's UN speech on 7 December 1988, three small defence plants were *totally* converted to civilian production in 1989. These are the Yoshkarola and Yuruzun plants and the Leninskaya Koznitsa naval shipyard in Kiev.[38] Even the most advanced defence factories are also being utilized to produce consumer goods. For example, the Khrunichev plant near Moscow, in addition to being one of the most sophisticated factories in the world for space technology, is now producing children's bicycles.[39]

More important will be the qualitative orientation. High-tech industrialization, in the form of automation, computerization and the use of micro-processors, is now a priority. Investment-intensive smoke-stack industries must give way to new technology. Four civilian machine-building industries were amalgamated with the Defence Ministry of the Electronics Industry to satisfy the demand for computerized equipment. Factory automation is now top priority, and almost every single new product entering into production contains micro-processors.

9. If military industries have lower priority for major intermediate inputs (electronic components and high-quality materials) then these can be provided to the civilian economy much faster. Endemic short-

---

[36] TASS interview with General A. Shabanov, *Daily Review* (Novosti Press), 27 Sep. 1989.

[37] See Anthony, I., Courades Allebeck, A., Gullikstad, E., Hagmeyer-Gaverus, G. and Wulf, H., 'Arms production', in SIPRI, *SIPRI Yearbook 1990: World Armaments and Disarmament* (Oxford University Press: Oxford, 1990), chapter 8.

[38] Vid, L., 'Guns into butter, Soviet style', *Bulletin of the Atomic Scientists*, Jan.–Feb. 1990, pp. 17–19.

[39] Steel, J., 'Glasnost comes to Soviet rocket factory', *The Guardian*, 21 Nov. 1989; Zakharchuk, M., 'The post office box: a view from inside', *Sotsialisticheskaya Industriya*, 23 May 1989, p. 2.

ages and input rationing will then be eased and a major impediment to inefficiency may be removed, making Soviet industry more competitive. One of the main reasons for the chronic shortages at the industrial level for the civilian industrial sector is the allocation structure. Both sectors compete directly for materials (steel, coal and construction stuff) and vital intermediates (ball-bearings and microelectronics). When there is an overall shortage and there is no market mechanism or price system to determine which enterprise should get the product first, the military industries have always had priority. Part of the inefficiency of Soviet civilian production is due to this factor. If the proposed transformations succeed, this allocation process will change.

10. The high-quality R&D and the large numbers of scientists and engineers employed in the defence sector can now be channelled to civilian sectors for the benefit of the economy as a whole.[40] By its own reckoning, in 1989 the USSR spent about 1.8 per cent of its GDP on military R&D. Using Western intelligence estimates, the proportion rises to 3.2 per cent. The corresponding figures for the USA are revealing. At the peak of military expenditure under the Reagan Administration, known for its encouragement of scientific innovation in the SDI programme, US military R&D amounted to about 0.8 per cent of the national output. Japan spends 0.01 per cent while the FRG spends 0.11 per cent of their respective national products. With a much smaller economic base, and a higher level of spending on military technology, the USSR simply cannot afford to be so wasteful, particularly as its civilian economy is known to be underdeveloped. Both in terms of the quality of research and the number of scientists and engineers employed, the loss to civil society must be immense. The 13 per cent cut in military R&D in 1989–90 is therefore an important step forward.

What is surprising is that in spite of past claims of the close integration of military and civilian production, and the use of 'dual-use technology', there seems to be very little interconnection between the two and few civilian spin-offs from defence R&D. It seems as if the

[40] The Sukhoi design bureau, known for the advanced fighters of the Su series, is increasingly moving into civilian aircraft design. It has designed a sports aeroplane, the Su-26M, and has plans (announced at the 1989 Paris air show) for a joint venture with the US firm Gulfstream to design and produce a supersonic business jet. See Cook, N., 'New challenges facing Soviet military industry', *Jane's Defence Weekly*, 16 Sep. 1989, pp. 507–509.

two industrial sectors have been hermetically sealed off from each other. President Gorbachev's warning about the existence of the Soviet Union's 'internal COCOM' [with reference to NATO's Coordinating Committee on Export Controls], which precludes advanced technology transfer from defence to civil industry, is a clear indication of the pervasiveness of this dichotomy. In his speech on 30 May 1989, in which he revealed Soviet military expenditure, he also said: 'Immense possibilities lie in using in the civilian sector the unique technology developed at the defence ministry enterprises. Conditions have been created today to put an end to the irrational secrecy, finishing up with with the so called internal COCOM'.[41]

Any relaxation of such restrictions is likely to increase productivity and introduce technological progress in the non-military sector similar to the levels attained in defence production.

The optimistic scenario sketched above, where *konversiya*, defined in the broadest sense, will be able to rejuvenate the economy, may not work out as planned. There are formidable structural and systemic weaknesses in the system which may hinder the transformation desired.

1. The amount of financial resources available from military expenditure (assuming that Soviet figures are correct) is rather small, particularly if compared to the astronomical budget deficit and the competing demands for governmental socio-economic spending.

2. There are significant short-term costs of demobilization and reduction or destruction of weapon stocks. Unemployed military officers are already complaining bitterly about the lack of opportunities and of amenities such as housing. The formation in 1989 of *Shchit* (Shield), the first Soviet military trade union,[42] is indicative of the armed forces' concern about their deteriorating position in society. Destruction of weapons, at the initial stages, can also be quite expensive.[43] Figures released during 1989 pertaining to disarmament provisions of the INF Treaty and to unilateral cuts are indicative of these costs.

---

[41] FBIS-SOV-89-103S (note 3).

[42] See Cornwell, R., 'Soviet soldiers left out in the cold', *The Independent*, 27 Nov. 1989. Criticism as well as spirited defence of the armed forces surfaced during a meeting of the Congress of People's Deputies; *The Guardian*, 31 May 1989. The problems of low-quality housing and housing shortages was voiced in *Moskovskiye Novosti* and reported in *Jane's Defence Weekly*, 8 July 1989, p. 38.

[43] See 'What's the price of blasting a missile?', *Krasnaya Zvezda*, 20 Oct. 1989.

3. The industrial organization structure required to extract the rewards of conversion may not yet be present in the Soviet Union. The leadership prefers existing arms factories to be converted into partial or full production of civilian goods. The alternative of transferring equipment and personnel to new or existing civilian factories is considered less desirable. Yet, the first option may be more expensive since new types of fixed cost will have to be incurred. It is thought that since military industries are inherently more efficient, converting existing facilities will in some sense carry over this efficiency to the production of new civilian products. This may not be the case. As discussed above, the high productivity of military industries was possible because they were insulated from the systemic weaknesses of the economy. They faced less shortages, had priority to high-quality input, paid lower prices for inputs and were covered by state subsidies if they failed to make adequate profits. Without such assistance their efficiency would be questionable. Changing over to civilian production will not alter these systemic weaknesses.

4. Since 1 January 1989, many military industries are operating under 'self-financing' (*khozraschet*). This has been the norm for civilian industry for some time but is new to the defence sector. It, too, will now be compelled to make profits and can no longer count on being bailed out in case of bankruptcy. As military industries begin producing consumer durables, competing on an open market, they may have to increase prices or lower quality to remain solvent and profitable.[44] Quality control is a perennial problem. Utilizing their monopoly, such industries can pass off sub-standard goods to consumers. If sub-standard components cannot be used for a defence product, a factory may use them for its civilian output.

5. The method of allowing military industries to take up civilian production does not tackle the basic problem of the Soviet 'internal COCOM'. The transfer of technology is still being internalized within the defence industrial ministries. Its effect could be described as that of a martial law for industry, with the efficient military system called in to sort out the difficulties of civilian society.[45] It is not surprising

---

[44] Kireyev, A., 'Restructuring the military-industrial complex', *New Times*, no. 36 (5–11 Sep. 1989), cited in *Strategic Review*, vol. 17, no. 4 (autumn 1989), pp. 83–84.

[45] Kireyev (note 44) states scathingly: 'The defense industry can, of course, fulfill the role of a fire brigade and put out, for a time, the seething discontent with the shortages of goods of prime necessity. But will it help to solve the problem completely? I am afraid it will not. By reducing the defense industry to an average and rather low level and making it produce kneading machines or electric shock guns for cattle slaughter, we are losing our last

that Colonel Professor Ivan Yudin has recalled the success of self-financing for military industries during the 'Great Patriotic War'.[46]

There can be little doubt that economic conversion from a military to a non-military mode of production will help the economy. The question is how large the beneficial effects will be and how long it will take to acquire the 'disarmament dividend'. Certainly in the long run, once the systemic problems discussed above are corrected, the economic effects of the transformation must be positive. Unfortunately, the leadership needs to show results quickly, particularly in the supply of consumption goods.

In terms of Soviet military expenditure, 1989 was a remarkable year. For the first time in two decades defence spending slowed down and was probably also reduced in real terms. Acquisition of military assets was being cut and procurement expenditure for the year was probably lower than for earlier years. There was also a promise of substantial future reductions in the pace of modernization, brought about by planned cuts in R&D spending. Large-scale conversion has been initiated, although it is still fraught with teething troubles. Uncertainties remain, but hopefully *glasnost* will dispel some of the opaqueness that still characterizes Soviet military expenditure. The Soviet military system is bound to become 'leaner'. Whether it will become 'meaner' is now purely a political question. The answer will depend on the success of the arms control process.

technological advantage'. See also Kireyev, A., 'What will global peace bring us?', *Pravda*, 14 Sep. 1989.
[46] Yudin, I., 'Defence industry and *khozraschet*', *Soviet Military Review*, no. 1 (Oct. 1989). The economics of military expenditure are discussed in Yudin, I., 'The effectiveness of using defence resources', *Soviet Military Review*, no. 12 (Dec. 1989).

7. The Asia–Pacific region: the emerging powers

I. New Soviet initiatives

The rapidly increasing economic power of the Far Eastern economies, as well as the rise of military expenditures coupled with major conflicts and security problems, have made the Asia–Pacific region extremely important. General Secretary Gorbachev's Vladivostok speech in July 1986[1] underscored the importance that the Soviet Union attaches to its role in this strategically crucial part of the world. In a sense, the Soviet proposals are a response to the substantial US presence in the region, but it is much more than that. A number of factors—economic, political and strategic—enhance the usefulness of the region to the USSR. These include the following: the growing economic importance of the eastern part of the country, as the repository of substantial natural resources; the necessity of using the Pacific Ocean, rather than the Baltic or the Mediterranean seas, as the conduit for trade and naval presence; the ability to trade with the future economic giants—China, Japan, the ASEAN (Association for South-East Asian) countries—and the newly industrializing countries—South Korea, Hong Kong and Taiwan; and finally, the desire for arms control measures and *détente* with China as a means to reduce defence spending.

In September 1988 Gorbachev reiterated the earlier initiatives and presented new proposals in another major speech, at Krasnoyarsk.[2] He proposed: no increase in nuclear weapons in the region; no increase in naval forces in the region; lowering military confrontations where the coasts of the USSR, China, Japan and the two Korean states converge; withdrawal of the USSR from its naval facilities in Viet Nam (Cam Ranh Bay) if the USA shuts down the Philippine bases; provision of safety for sea channels and air communications; an international

---

[1] 'Text of the Vladivostok speech', *News and Views of the USSR*, Soviet Embassy, Washington, DC, 1986. For a critical commentary, see Kapista, M., 'Paths to peace and security in the Asia and Pacific region', *International Affairs* (Moscow), no. 8 (Aug. 1987), pp. 27–37.
[2] *The Times*, 17 Sep. 1988. For recent diplomatic efforts, see also Gourlay, R., in *Financial Times*, 31 May 1988.

conference on the Indian Ocean as a zone of peace; and creation of a regional negotiating machinery (possibly along the lines of negotiations for Europe) for confidence-building measures. He also suggested that the three major powers should start preliminary discussions on these matters. All of these could have an impact on regional military spending, which is high.

In his 1988 United Nations speech as well, Gorbachev attributed significant importance to the region, particularly with respect to troops on the Sino-Soviet border. He offered a unilateral 200 000 reduction in troops and corresponding assets; the Soviet presence in neighbouring Mongolia would also be reduced significantly. All of these were favourable and extremely generous signals towards a peaceful settlement of long-standing disputes.

The USSR already has a substantial naval presence in the area. The Soviet Pacific Fleet of the Far Eastern Strategic Theatre (with headquarters at Vladivostok) is the largest of its fleets, with more than 200 combatant ships (major and minor) and over 100 submarines and 2 carriers. The US naval superiority in the region, to which the USSR tries to respond, is overwhelming: the Pacific Fleet (with headquarters at Pearl Harbour) contains the 6th and the 7th Fleets with six or seven carrier battle groups.

Regional military expenditures are also significant and rising rapidly. SIPRI estimates show that in the mid-1980s about 10 per cent of the world total was being spent by the countries in the Asia–Pacific region; this was the highest regional concentration of defence spending. Growth rates have also been high. Between 1980 and 1985, the total combined military expenditures of Japan, the ASEAN countries, the two Korean states and Taiwan rose by almost 4 per cent per annum in real terms. This trend was maintained, and exceeded, in the late 1980s. Although the reported military budget of the People's Republic of China has fallen (see below) the lack of proper data makes it difficult to assess its true impact. However, Chinese arms modernization continues, and China does have a formidable military capability in terms of its arsenal as well as being the second nuclear weapon power in the region.

Soviet perceptions of and attitudes towards the two major local powers, China and Japan, are somewhat different. For China, a *rapprochement* is at hand after the 1989 summit meeting between Gorbachev and China's then paramount leader Deng Xiaoping. In

1990, Premier Lin Peng visited the Soviet Union; this was the first visit of such a senior official in three decades. The relations between Moscow and Tokyo are fraught with more problems. Three elements define the parameters of this relationship.

1. The geo-strategic position of Japan makes it a crucial player. Not only does it lie to the eastern seaboard of the USSR, but it also provides basing rights (which may have offensive capabilities) to the USA; much more important is its control of the vital outlets for the Soviet Navy to the Pacific Ocean in the form of the Straits of Soya, Nemuro, Tsugaru and Tsushima.[3]

2. Given the close relations between Japan and the USA, as well as Moscow's own intransigence in negotiating outstanding territorial problems, the USSR has tried to keep political and economic factors as separate as possible. Thus it refuses to discuss the Northern Territories which Japan alleges are occupied. On the other hand it wishes to broaden trade horizons.

3. The USSR believes that Japanese technology and investment could be essential for the development of Siberia.[4] In a sense, the economic miracles of the Pacific region have passed the USSR by, and it would like to reap the spin-offs, particularly in terms of technology imports and the financing of regional development. Japanese credits could be as desirable in the East as recent German credits have been in the West.

It has been claimed that optimally the USSR would like to 'Findlandize' Japan[5] and use the resultant neutrality to maximum advantage in terms of economic, trade and technological relationships without fears of military problems. Whatever the true intentions, it seems that such a step is no longer feasible, given Japan's pre-eminence in the Western economic world. The economic muscle will eventually lead to political power, and the sort of subsidiary role envisaged in the above model can no longer apply. Further, as discussed below, Japanese defence spending and capability are also increasing.

[3] Chi Young Pak, *The Korean Straits* (Martinus Nijhoff Publishers: Dordrecht, 1988) reviews the wide-ranging naval problems in East Asia.

[4] *USSR Yearbook '88* (Novosti: Moscow, 1988) gives an account of the comprehensive economic development plans for the Siberian region.

[5] See Tokinoya, A., *The Japan–US Alliance: A Japanese Perspective*, Adelphi Papers 212 (International Institute for Strategic Studies: London, 1986).

Overall, the Soviet initiatives for the Asia–Pacific region need to be taken seriously. In terms of economic performance as well as security perceptions, this area will continue to increase in prominence. Its problems and characteristics—high growth, increasing international integration, flashpoints of armed conflicts, intertwined domestic and external security factors, the co-existence of opposing social systems and superpower involvement—are not dissimilar to Europe in the 1950s and 1960s. Policy dilemmas and their solutions, for early in the next century, need to be considered now.

II. China

Major economic reforms have been initiated in China, and throughout the 1980s the marketization of the economy continued with speed. Initial successes, in releasing the productive potential of the economy, were astounding. The GNP doubled during the decade, with agriculture and industry both notching up high growth rates. Export-promoting industrialization earned substantial foreign exchange and had a multiplier effect on productive capacity. Major structural reforms were introduced: the family contract system in agriculture and reduced mandatory state procurement, allowing more sales to the open market; reduction of the influence of the planning authorities in enterprise management and the use of self-financing; decontrol of many prices; linking pay to productivity; creation of Special Economic Zones for foreign trade and investment; and encouragement of small private businesses in the service sector of the rural economy. However, inflation and overheating of the economy have always been a major problem. By the turn of the decade inflation was above 20 per cent, and serious structural problems, arising from an excessively high rate of growth, provoked a contractionary fiscal and monetary policy. This has caused a recession, and growth rates will need to be slowed down considerably.

Chinese military expenditure, and the weapon procurement process, is essentially dependent on the will of the political authorities and on economic constraints. Political perceptions in turn are related to domestic control in a party-dominated hierarchical system as well as threat perceptions in a world dominated by two superpowers who have never been truly friendly with the country. This evaluation remains true today as it was in 1949 when China was founded. It is also not easy to categorize China. In terms of per capita income and levels of development it remains a Third World country;[6] as an actor on the international arena—and in particular in terms of its security policies—it is a major power. China is one of five countries in the world with a strategic nuclear force; it is a permanent member of the UN Security Council; it is a major arms exporter, utilizing arms transfers both as a foreign policy tool and as an earner of foreign exchange; and it has contributed to the proliferation of ballistic missiles—yet it is the only major power whose military expenditure has consistently declined throughout the decade.

Many of these factors played a role in forming developments in China in 1989. President Gorbachev's historic visit to Beijing in May 1989 signalled the beginning of a new phase in Sino-Soviet relations, after three decades of hostility. The three main obstacles to *détente*—boundary disputes, Soviet support for Viet Nam and the Soviet invasion of Afghanistan—were addressed, mainly as a result of Soviet initiatives. International relations between the two major socialist powers are at their best for many years, although China is wary of the political reforms in the USSR as well as the nationality problems. At the same time as inter-state disputes were being resolved, however, China suffered an acute domestic political crisis, culminating in the brutal use of military force in Tiananmen Square in June 1989 to suppress a popular movement for democratic reforms and political pluralism. The importance attached to the armed forces in quelling the democratic movement prompted fears that the influence of the military was increasing and that defence spending could rise in the future as a 'payment' for the military's support of the political leadership.[7] These fears were realized by the publication of the state budget for 1990, which reversed a 10-year downward trend and increased defence spending substantially. More important, the share of the defence sector in total central government expenditure, which represents the political preferences of the authorities, rose by a large amount.

After the revelations regarding Soviet military expenditures, China became the only major power that still provides little information except a single-line entry in the annual state budget about defence spending, made public only since the late 1970s. More general

[6] World Bank, *World Development Report 1989* (Oxford University Press: New York, 1989).
[7] 'Tiananmen 1989: a symposium', *Problems of Communism*, Sep.–Oct. 1989.

qualitative information is slowly becoming available so it is difficult to see why there is such obsessive secrecy about financial data, particularly the allocation of the stated amount into its constituent parts. It is widely believed that the defence budget gives only a fraction of total military spending, the rest coming from other budgetary accounts, and does not take into account the revenues raised by the People's Liberation Army (PLA) itself. Even a PLA official has claimed that the state defence budget is about 70 per cent of total spending and that the remaining 30 per cent is earned elsewhere.[8]

This type of secrecy often leads to contradictory evaluations of the Chinese military capability which is portrayed as having both a formidable and an obsolete defence capability. In the same way, the defence forces are claimed to be modernized as well as depleted. Overseas press reports state that military R&D alone is twice that of the official total defence budget;[9] the Chinese press claim that the PLA accounts for 10 per cent of the world's armed forces but only 1.6 per cent of world military expenditure.[10] It is possible that all of these claims are partially true. However, it would help the analysts, and improve China's international image, if the government provided more information, at least at the level that the USSR has done in recent years. The discussion that follows is therefore tentative and based mainly on Western analysis.

SIPRI estimates show that actual Chinese military expenditure in 1988/89 could have exceeded 40 billion yuan, almost double the official figure, amounting to almost 4 per cent of national income and 15 per cent of central government expenditure.

The main feature of the Chinese armed forces is the slow but resolute modernization that is continuing in spite of financial stringency. In 1988, it was announced that a new advanced fighter had entered service, possibly the J-8II.[11] The Xia Class SSBN gives it a major naval strategic capability and allows it more power projection as an impending blue-water navy. Reports of more such SSBNs being

[8] *Ming Bao*, 24 Apr. 1988, quoted in Lin, C. Z., 'Employment implications of defence cutbacks in China', World Employment Programme Research Working Paper, International Labour Organization, Geneva, 1989.

[9] *Far Eastern Economic Review*, 24 Mar. 1988, p. 66.

[10] *Beijing Review*, vol. 31, no. 45 (7–13 Nov. 1988).

[11] *Jiefangjun Bao* [Liberation Daily], 7 Oct. 1988, p. 1, quoted in Dreyer, J. T., 'The PLA in 1988: an overview', in ed. R. H. Yang, *SCPS Yearbook on PLA Affairs, 1988/89* (Sun Yat-sen Centre for Policy Studies: Taiwan, 1989), p. 4.

constructed abound, although the process has slowed down due to shortage of funds. Rumours continue that China intends to build its first aircraft-carrier, although these are yet to be verified. Certainly China's naval doctrines claim that the power of the modern navy depends on *liangjian yiting* (two surface combatants and one submarine). The surface ships referred to are the aircraft-carrier and the guided missile cruiser.[12]

Historical evolution of defence spending

The withdrawal of Soviet military assistance and technicians in 1960, as well as the disrupting economic effects of the Great Leap Forward initiated by Chairman Mao Zedong in 1958, adversely affected the Chinese military in the early 1960s to a large extent. However, by the late 1960s the military establishment had gained ascendancy. Defence spending rose rapidly during the 1960s for a number of reasons: US involvement in the Viet Nam War; clashes with Soviet troops along the border at the Ussuri and Amur rivers; the importance of Defence Minister Lin Biao in the political hierarchy as the heir-designate of Mao; and the expansion of the defence industrial base into the central remote regions of the country to prepare for 'total war'. According to the official budget, military spending rose nearly threefold during 1961 and 1970. Both Chinese estimates and those of the US Defense Intelligence Agency claim that a peak was reached in 1971. In that year Lin Biao was killed in a mysterious aeroplane crash, the Cultural Revolution (1966–76) was at its disruptive peak, and the initial *rapprochement* began with the USA (through Nixon's visit to Beijing) after more than two decades. All of these factors caused military spending to fall for a few years. The next peak was attained in 1979 when China fought a bloody war with socialist united Viet Nam, its erstwhile friend.

In December 1978, the 3rd Plenum of the 11th Central Committee of the CPC (Communist Party of China) established a wide-ranging scheme of reforms and principles which would profoundly shape the course of post-Maoist China. All aspects of political and economic life were affected, and the military were not immune to these forces of change. Deng Xiaoping, later to become paramount leader of China,

[12] Lee, N., *China's Defence Modernization and Military Leadership* (Australian National University Press: Sydney, 1989), pp. 196–97.

seized the initiative and resurrected the concept of the 'Four Modernizations'—that of industry, agriculture, science and technology, and defence, in that order. Economic growth, market-oriented reforms, decentralization of decision making, opening up to the rest of the world with vigorous growth in foreign trade as well as increases in technological sophistication would be the order of the day. Even though the military establishment was not left out of the scheme for rejuvenation, it was clearly awarded the lowest priority. Rather a reverse causation was established: the defence sector would not be able to perform its functions adequately with a modern efficient force unless there was economic development in general. The overriding concern was rapid growth, which would bring one of the poorest countries in the world to developed-nation status by the turn of the century. In the absence of major security threats, economically 'unproductive' expenditure on defence would have to be curtailed and the resources utilized to achieve economic development and social welfare.

The DIA has made independent estimates of Chinese defence spending for the years 1967–83.[13] According to these *estimates* military spending in real terms rose by over 14 per cent per annum between 1967 and 1971. It fell by 6.5 per cent per year in 1971–73 and then rose steadily. Between 1973 and 1979, the peak dictated by the Viet Nam War, the growth was around 4.7 per cent per annum. This source also states that in 1979 defence expenditure was 46 billion yuan, in 1974 prices. Translated into 1988 prices this figure would be 91 billion yuan, a very high figure indeed. As a method of comparison it can be noted that the US intelligence estimate of China's defence spending in current prices for 1988 is approximately 45 billion yuan.[14] If these figures are of the right order of magnitude, China almost halved its defence spending between 1979 and 1988.

[13] Parris, E. 'China's defence expenditure', in US Congress, Joint Economic Committee, *China's Economy Looks Toward the Year 2000*, vol. 2 (US Government Printing Office, Washington, DC, 1986), pp. 148–68.

[14] 'The Chinese economy in 1988 and 1989: reform on hold, economic problems mount', a report by the CIA presented to the Subcommittee on Technology and National Security of the Joint Economic Committee, 7 July 1989, mimeo.

Current military expenditure

After the publication in 1989 of credible Soviet defence expenditure figures, China is now the only major country in the world which still refuses to allow an inspection of its defence spending. Very little is known from open sources about the absolute level of Chinese military expenditure—the sole source of official information is a single-line entry in the state budget bearing the title 'defence'. There is some evidence that China uses the Soviet method of national accounting,[15] concealing military spending in much the same way as is done in the Soviet budget. The published budget would then include personnel costs and operation and maintenance (O&M), while procurement, investment in weapon industries (all run by the government) and R&D would be left out. The net material product (NMP) accounts have three broad components: consumption, social consumption and accumulation. Defence spending on food, clothing, fuel, maintenance, and so on, would fall in the first two categories, while expenditure on weapon procurement (including construction) could be listed under the latter. Military R&D may be subsumed under more general research expenditure as part of the science budget.

According to recent Chinese publications, the PLA budget has 11 principal categories: living expenses; official business; operating expenses; education and training; equipment purchases; maintenance; capital construction; scientific research; combat-readiness expenses; external affairs; and expenses relating to preparing for emergencies. It is curious that forces' pay (military, paramilitary, civilians and reserves) is not mentioned at all except tangentially in the first category. This is probably the reason why a recent Western European Union report implied that personnel costs are not included in the defence budget.[16] Yet, this runs contrary to what is known of socialist national accounting. Instead, it is equally probable that weapon procurement is hidden in accounts for industry and accumulation of reserves. This practice could only have increased under the civilianization programme through conversion, where it is now difficult to distinguish between the types of sales (civil or military) of the defence industries. Estimation problems are compounded by the

[15] Crane, K., *Military Spending in Eastern Europe,* Prepared for the Office of the Under Secretary of Defense, Rand Report (Rand Corp.: Santa Monica, Calif., 1987).
[16] *Western European Security: Defence Implications of the People's Republic of China's Evolving Geopolitical Situation,* Report of the Assembly of the Western European Union, 6 Nov. 1989 (Western European Union: Paris, 1989).

fact that the PLA is allowed to keep a part of the foreign exchange earnings from overseas sales of Chinese weapons to put towards its own procurement programmes. Reports vary about the actual proportion; it could be anything between 40 and 80 per cent, but it is certainly significant. It has been claimed that in 1987 arms sales to Iran accounted for almost $1 billion. If a large part of this was diverted to the PLA, its procurement spending could be boosted significantly, but these amounts probably would never appear in the defence budget.

Nevertheless, there is little doubt that Chinese military expenditure has been declining in real terms, at least until 1990, and definitely as a percentage of its national output. The reduction has been made possible by a cut in forces by over one million men, postponing some modernization, slowing down plans for an expansion towards a blue-water navy, using revenues from arm sales to finance imports of weapon technology which can be adapted to local use, producing their own food, doing contract work—such as in construction—for civilian sectors and launching a major programme of industrial conversion using spare capacity of the defence industrial base to produce civilian goods which can be sold for profit.[17]

The pragmatic leadership no longer believes in the 'inevitability' of major wars even though regional and localized conflicts will remain (as the skirmishes with Viet Nam show). Normalization of relations with the USSR continues satisfactorily. With a few notable exceptions, its security relationships with neighbours are good or improving. However, the most important reason for the reduction seems to be the demands of domestic economic and political reforms, which require more resources to be released to the civilian economy together with a new type of armed force vastly different from the traditional norms of the PLA.

Troop reductions for the PLA, arms modernization, significant organizational changes including reorganization of military regions, and employing civilians in general headquarters are all measures designed to create a more professional force structure. An interesting development in 1988, equally important for its symbolic value as for

---

[17] Klintworth, G., *China's Modernization: The Strategic Implications for the Asian–Pacific Region* (Australian Government Publishing Service: Canberra, 1989). See also Lathan, R. J., 'China's defence industrial policy: looking towards the year 2000', and Liu, C., 'A preliminary study on the defence economy of the PRC: past, present and towards the year 2000', in ed. Yang (note 11), pp. 79–94 and 95–106.

its military usefulness, was the restoration of the ranking system originally abolished by Chairman Mao Zedong.[18] The year also saw the beginnings of a local version of a rapid deployment force, airborne troops capable of rapid military responses; the *Liberation Army Daily* calls it the 'fist platoon'.[19]

The changes that are taking place are partly related to the structural transformation in military doctrine and strategy that followed the abandonment of the Maoist concept of 'people's war'. This traditional concept envisaged a massive armed force, helped by large reserves and supported by the population at large. Modern weapons were less important compared to the will of the army to resist conventional attacks. Nuclear forces would be used only as a last recourse and purely for retaliatory self-defence. The new theory, 'people's war under modern conditions',[20] relies much more on weapon modernization, professional armed forces, forward defence and limited aggression where necessary.

However, once again, as elsewhere, the fundamental reasons for arms control are related to economic and technological structural changes that are taking place in the society and economy. In the face of intense competition for resources, the government simply cannot afford large-scale increases in defence spending as was the practice in the past. The share of the defence budget in the total has declined, according to official statistics, from over 15 per cent in the early 1980s to around 8 per cent in 1989. At the same time, the aggregate budget deficit has risen from less than 3 billion yuan (in 1982) to over 8 billion yuan in 1988. China's foreign debt is also in the big league; its current level is around $30 billion, about 10 per cent of its GNP.

The economic nexus of China's arms production and exports is crucial in understanding the country's military expenditure process. The foreign exchange made available through weapon sales is used to finance force modernization at home. This helps, partially, to keep domestic defence spending low; thereby, potentially valuable resources are released for other needs of higher social priority. Traditionally, China has been adept at 'learning by doing'; this entails adapting technology through indigenous efforts to suit their own

---

[18] *The Guardian*, 2 Aug. 1988, p. 8; see also *Asian Security 1988–89* (Brassey's: London, 1988), p. 67.

[19] *The Guardian*, 2 Aug. 1988.

[20] For a description of Chinese military philosophy and details of their arms conversion plans, see Dassu, M., 'The problem of reconversion of the military industry: the case of China' (del Centro studi di politica internazionale (CeSPI): Rome, 1988), mimeo.

needs. Now they are gaining expertise in 'learning by window-shopping'. China has not bought many actual weapon systems from abroad. What it really needs is technology which can be useful for domestic production. It also saves costs owing to savings on expensive R&D. China has learned a lot from studying the blueprints of eager sellers (the so-called 'window-shopping') and then ingeniously adapting the knowledge to its own requirements. Wherever expensive technology has to be actually paid for, it has utilized the revenue from arms sales, thus restraining its actual military burden.

The evolution of the official budget, although not the precise figure, gives a good enough time trend of the changes in military expenditure that reflected the mood of the leadership around 1980. Table 7.1 gives data for defence spending (in current and constant prices) as well as its share in central government expenditure, to reflect its political priority. Between 1979 and 1981, military expenditure in real terms declined sharply by 30 per cent. Both investment and operating costs fell rapidly, but R&D remained stable. The share in the central government budget also fell from over 17 per cent to around 15 per cent.

In spite of far-reaching economic reforms and the rapid transformation of the Chinese economy in the first half of the 1980s, it was not easy to continuously reduce defence spending to support the transfer of resources from the military to the civilian sectors. Between 1981 and 1984 military expenditure did not fall, even though exhortations were made for the defence sector to make the requisite sacrifices. By 1985, however, Chairman Deng was sufficiently powerful to order major cutbacks, particularly in the level of forces. The PLA was to reduce its troop levels by one million men, a cut of 20–25 per cent. Procurement expenditure would be correspondingly reduced. In addition, the defence industrial conversion to civilian production, started earlier, would be speeded up.

By around 1988–89 the process was almost complete. As table 7.1 shows, official military expenditure fell in real terms by over 20 per cent; so also did the share in the state budget, to about 8 per cent— probably the lowest in modern Chinese history. Unfortunately, 1990 has seen an upward movement once again. Whether this a trend, or a temporary phenomenon, is as yet unknown.

Table 7.1. Official Chinese defence spending, 1975–90

Year	Milex, current (b. yuan)	Share of CGE[a] (%)	Share of NI[b] (%)	Milex, constant (b. 1988 yuan)
1975	14.25	*17.4*	*6.7*	27.88
1976	13.45	*16.7*	*5.5*	25.92
1977	14.90	*17.7*	*5.6*	28.33
1978	16.78	*15.1*	*5.6*	31.65
1979	22.27	*17.5*	*6.7*	41.17
1980	19.38	*16.0*	*5.3*	33.37
1981	16.80	*15.1*	*4.3*	28.20
1982	17.64	*15.3*	*4.1*	29.02
1983	17.71	*13.7*	*3.7*	28.60
1984	18.08	*11.7*	*3.2*	28.41
1985	19.15	*10.4*	*2.7*	26.91
1986	20.13	*8.6*	*2.6*	26.43
1987	20.98	*8.6*	*2.3*	25.32
1988	21.80	*8.1*	*1.9*	21.80
1989	24.55*c*	*8.4*	*1.9*	20.46
1990	28.90*c*	*11.5*	..	23.10

a CGE: central government expenditure.
b NI: national income.
c Planned figure.

Source: SIPRI data base; authors' estimates.

No figures whatsoever are available from official sources regarding Chinese procurement expenditures. The PLA routinely keeps large inventories of weapon assets: currently, over 10 000 tanks, about 3000 APCs and around 4000 fighters. However, much of this equipment is old and does not indicate annual acquisition. It is believed that procurement spending has also displayed a downward trend during the 1980s, and the rate of decline is similar to overall expenditures. A recent report claims weapon spending to be around 5 billion yuan, about a quarter of the official budget; but this seems to be very low, particularly since the budget itself under-reports actual military expenditure.

A more revealing way of understanding Chinese procurement policy is to study the defence industry in China. Much less work has been done in this field in the West compared to the Soviet industry, and very few studies have emanated from the country itself in the past. Perceptions may be changing, however, particularly as China increasingly opens up to the West; in addition, the export of arms requires more publicity regarding capabilities. *China Today: Aviation Industry*,[21] gives a wealth of information, from indigenous sources, on aircraft manufacturing

Defence industry and conversion

China produces the whole gamut of modern weapons—from guns to ICBMs. In terms of its potential output it has one of the largest defence industries in the world. According to some analysts, the Chinese defence industry is the third largest in the world, after those of the USSR and the USA. With the indigenous capability to equip the second largest standing armed force in the world, in addition to equipping a strategic nuclear force, the extent of defence industrialization cannot be questioned.

On the other hand, the technological sophistication is considered to be extremely low, with second-hand designs adapted from the 1950s and 1960s as a base for production. For example, in the early 1980s it was claimed: 'China continues to produce . . . aircraft that are technological inferior and obsolete when compared to their counterpart aircraft of both Soviet and Free World manufacture'.[22]

In recent years two predominant characteristics are evident.

1. Given stringent resource constraints, a slow but steady modernization, including technology transfer, is taking place. Although uneven, dictated by funding problems and the availability of suitable dual-use technology, China hopes by the turn of the decade to acquire a smaller but more capable armed force. Arms exports, in addition to their political leverage, have provided substantial foreign exchange, which has traditionally been a bottleneck.

2. A major programme of industrial conversion is taking place in China, which was the first country in the world to operationalize the 'swords into ploughshares' concept by physically restructuring its defence plants.

---

[21] *China Today: Aviation Industry*, China Today Series (Chinese Social Science Press: Beijing, 1989).

[22] Statement by Major General S. Bissell, Deputy Director DIA on the Allocation of Resources in the Soviet Union and China—1983, before the Subcommittee on International Trade, Finance and Security Economics of the Joint Economic Committee, US Congress, 28 June 1983, p. 103, mimeo.

The historical evolution of the Chinese defence industry can be divided into three epochs: close Sino-Soviet co-operation which abruptly ended in 1960; a long period (until the late 1970s) characterized by adaptation, attempts at producing indigenous technology, 'learning by doing', minimal but crucial technology transfers, various forms of political disruptions and slow progress characterized by significant failures; and finally, since the early 1980s the industry has entered a phase of rationalization, modernization and technology imports, arms exports and major conversion. As is clear from the contradictory nature of the evolution, it is not easy to construct a framework to deal with this industry.

After the experience of the Korean War the government moved rapidly to construct a defence industry with Soviet help. In 1953 an agreement was signed for setting up 143 major co-operative projects (which later became 156). Most of the technology transfer (such as the main battle tank, the T-54 or the fighters of the early MiG series) took place during this period, and the foundations for a very large industrial base were laid.

The departure of Soviet technicians and technology in 1960 was a painful experience for the new industry. In addition, the disruptive industrial effects of the politico-economic reforms, such as the Great Leap Forward or the Cultural Revolution, affected industrialization. As China became more isolationist throughout the 1960s, the development of indigenous technology and import-substituting industrialization was stressed. This was achieved at great cost, in both human and other resources, but technological obsolescence threatened to wipe out the modest gains.

In the mid-1960s a remarkable geographical and regional transformation of the defence industrial base took place. Hitherto, most of the factories and plants were based in the coastal areas and immediately behind them. The most important aircraft factory, for example, was at Shenyang (producing the J-series fighters) in the north-east. Under the orders of Mao, a massive diversification took place to the interior of the country, centred around Chongquing in Sichuan province in the south-west of the country. This huge region, taking in the provinces of Sichuan and Guizhou, the southern parts of Shaanxi and Gansi, as well as the western parts of Hunan and Hubei, became what has been called the Third Capital Construction Front, or the Third Line Construction.[23]

Relocation and reconstruction to the Third Line were motivated by Mao's doctrine of total war, when it was anticipated that the central region would be self-sufficient to meet a wartime situation including a strategic nuclear attack, even if the more advanced coastal regions succumbed. There was also the belief that spin-off from technologically advanced defence industrialization would affect the backward regions which constituted the Third Line. Be that as it may, an enormous effort was made to build almost from scratch a whole defence industrial base for the Army and the Air Force, producing almost the whole product range from tanks to fighters.

The amount of resources expended on this region in general, as well as for the defence industry in particular, was truly astounding. Almost 40 per cent of national investment during the 3rd and 4th Five-Year Plans (1966–75) was poured into this area which traditionally had received only about one-fourth of the total. The share of defence investment was even higher. An astonishing 93.4 per cent of total investment in the aviation industry during the 3rd FYP went to the Third Line Construction. During the 4th FYP the share was nearly as high, or 83.2 per cent. 'Large numbers of factory plants were constructed in the third line during those ten years. A group of enterprises and administrative organizations including aircraft and engine factories, accessory factories, special factories and design institutes, warehouses, hospitals and schools were set up in the remote strategic Guizhou area and mountainous area in south Shaanxi Province. . . . Marching into the third line, (defence) industry had brought water, electricity, transportation, school, department stores and modern information of economy, technology and culture to remote areas, supported remote area construction and hence, accelerated the change of situation to those industrially and economically weak areas'.[24]

From the early 1970s China began to open up, but very cautiously, to the rest of the world. A major development was licensed production using Western technology. In the mid-1970s the manufacturing licence for the Spey MK 202 turbofan engine was purchased from Rolls Royce in Britain and called the WS9 and produced in the Xian plant (originally used by the Ministry of Defence for the F-4 Phantom

[23] See Lin (note 8) for a comprehensive account of defence industrialization and conversion at the Third Line.
[24] See note 21, pp. 63–64.

fighters then).[25] But such major technology purchases were un-common, and self-reliance was still the order of the day, at least until the end of the Maoist era.

The third phase has seen China as a bigger importer of technology to help in the modernization of the defence industry, even though the fundamentals of self-reliance will remain. The major restraints are from suppliers (the USA, for example, banned military-related sales after the Tiananmen Square massacres) as well as the perennial problem of foreign exchange. In 1988 there were reports of US avionics being purchased for the advanced J-8II fighters and of collaboration with France and Australia to produce a new helicopter.

Throughout the 1980s modernization and resource constraints have both been stressed. To reconcile the two, the armed forces have not generally introduced a new generation of equipment. Rather, the emphasis has been to upgrade and modernize existing equipment. Considerable successes have been reported, particularly in upgrading the main battle tanks, fighters and some types of naval vessel. It is also worth stressing that R&D expenditure was the only category of resources in military expenditure which consistently increased in real terms over the decade. Today, Chinese defence industries and their products are still backward compared to other major powers, but they are definitely not obsolete. In this respect there is a close similarity between civilian and military industrialization, which is not surprising for a dual economy such as China's, continuing with a modified version of import-substituting industrialization and trying to move on to the next phase of export-promoting industrialization.

The unprecedented scale of conversion initiated by the authorities also emphasizes the close nexus between the civilian and military sectors. It includes not only industrial conversion but also, similar to the USSR, a restructuring of the armed forces. There are many facets of this transformation: reduction of military manpower and transfer to civilian employment; military factories producing consumer goods; army welfare installations, such as hospitals and schools, opening up to the general public; the sale of services such as warehouse storage and ship's space for transportation; growing of own food and producing clothing for internal use; and advanced R&D, particularly in space technology and computers, being increasingly diverted to

---

[25] See note 21, p. 221.

non-military uses. Overall, the sheer scale of the undertaking is mind-boggling.

Clearly, there have been problems. The reduction of manpower was very large indeed, particularly since there was high unemployment in China in 1985. The transitory cost of absorbing these people into the industrial labour force was high. China also suffered from open unemployment as a result of its market-oriented economic policy. In addition, there were financial costs, as industrial plants had to be retooled and new machinery installed. In the Third Line alone, over 2 billion yuan was allocated to restructure and relocate defence plants. It has been stated officially that 1 billion yuan was allocated for housing and re-settlement of demobilized personnel after the major cut in forces beginning in 1985. Clearly, the Ministry of National Defence was not spending these huge sums of money, and the costs were borne by the budget elsewhere.

Charges of corruption are rampant, as the armed forces try to make indiscriminate profits out of sales of army surplus products. The military itself are worried that their modernization programme may suffer as greater attention is paid to earning profits. Industrial workers in the defence establishment also fear loss of privileges and in the worst case redundancy through bankruptcy. In spite of these problems, however, the progress of restructuring seems to be going fairly well.

There are many reports about the consumer goods produced by the military: by 1983, over two million bicycles, almost one and a half million sewing machines, about two million fans and 70 per cent of all motorcycles produced in the country came from defence establishments. Fighter jet factories produce rubbish compactors, ordnance factories make fertilizers, and factories producing uniforms now also make T-shirts.

In addition, the armed forces are cultivating more of their own food (200 new farms produce 500 million kg); they are operating mines (the value of output is 700 million yuan); services hospitals are open to the general public (43 million patients in 1985–87); and a PLA trading organization runs hotels and plans to open a Ramada Inn as a joint venture.[26]

It is not easy to get precise and consistent figures about what proportion of defence industry capacity or output is transferred to

[26] See Lin (note 8).

civilian production. Chinese estimates have routinely claimed that 40–50 per cent of military industrial capacity could be used for civilian output. In 1990, an overseas estimate gave a figure of 80 per cent, which seems palpably high.[27] The most reasonable seems to be the Xinhua report, which states that civilian products' proportion in total defence industries' output rose from 8.1 per cent in 1979 to 60 per cent in 1989,[28] a staggering increase indeed. Consistent financial figures are even more difficult to come by. One estimate suggests that the total value of such output was 20 billion yuan in 1989.[29]

Finally, no discussion of the Chinese defence industrial base is complete without some analysis of its central organizational structure, since in a planned economy this feature can play an important role in pointing out the goals of the system. Until the late 1970s the defence plants and industries were grouped under the Ministries of Machine Building or the Ministries of Machine Industries (MMI). In this period there were eight such MMIs, numerically called First through to Eighth. The first was for civilian machineries while the others dealt consecutively with nuclear, aircraft, electronics, munitions, shipbuilding, missiles and space. After reorganization in the early 1980s, names were also given to ministries instead of numbers, reported as the Nuclear, Aviation (Aeronautics), Electronics, Ordnance, and Space (Astronautics) Industry Ministries as well as the China State Shipbuilding Corporation (CSSC). In 1986, to facilitate civilian control as well as to help technology transfer and conversion, the organizations were put under the direct control of the State Council alone and no longer run jointly with the Central Military Commission.

A final major organizational change, this time towards more commercialization, was the creation in the 1980s of a number of major corporations which handle the production and particularly the foreign sale of their defence industries' respective output. These are: China North Industries Corporation (NORINCO, now called NORIN), responsible for ordnance, ammunitions, and so on; the China Precision Machinery Import–Export Corporation (CPMIEC), responsible for guided missiles; CSSC, as mentioned above, ships; China Electronic Import–Export Corporation (CEIEC), electronic

[27] *Far Eastern Economic Review*, vol. 148, no. 14 (5 Apr. 1990), p. 28, quotes Chinese officials.
[28] Xinhua press report, 3 Feb. 1990, translation in *IDSA News Review on East Asia*, vol. 3, no. 3 (Mar. 1990), p. 253.
[29] See note 27.

equipment; the China Aviation Technology Import–Export Corporations (CATIC), aircraft; the China Nuclear Energy Industrial Corporation (CNEIC), nuclear energy and weapons; and the China Great Wall Industrial Corporation (CGWIC), space technology. It should be emphasized that these corporations are responsible for both military and civilian products, wherever applicable, within their respective jurisdictions.

There have been reports that further reorganization is continuing. For example, in 1988 it was reported that the defence ministry of ordnance industry and the civilian ministry of the machine building (mechanical) industry were being integrated into the China Mechanical Industrial Commission (CMIC) which will also control both NORIN as well as having major civilian function of selling engineering products. More organizational changes are under way.

These structural changes are meant to move the industry from centralization and concentration (in the hands of the central Ministry of National Defence) to commercialization and conversion. The idea is to make them more flexible and efficiency-oriented rather than being over-bloated with large surplus capacity as so often happened in the past.

Nowhere is the successful commercialization of the Chinese arms industry as evident as in the international arms trade in the 1980s. Until then China provided small quantities of arms, strictly for political purposes, often to counter the influence of the USSR, and usually as foreign military assistance. Taking advantage of the Iraq–Iran War, China became a major arms merchant, quadrupling (in volume terms) its foreign sales. All of it went to the Third World for obvious reasons: cheap price, rugged usage, high quality for low-intensity conflicts, easy operationability—all of these features made these weapons useful to developing countries.

China has also sold sophisticated weapons to particularly Iran and Iraq during their long war. Maximum attention has been focused on missiles, specifically the Silkworm, which was used extensively in the 'war of the cities'—Baghdad and Teheran. The most notorious, however, was the sale of IRBMs to Saudi Arabia (called the DF-3 or CSS-2). Many countries, including the USSR and India, consider this threatening and destabilizing, particularly if they are armed with non-conventional weapons (chemical, biological and nuclear). It is true that Saudi Arabia has promised to utilize only conventional weapons

Table 7.2. China's arms exports, 1981–88

Index: 1981 = 100

Year	SIPRI	CRS	ACDA
1981	100	100	100
1982	240	291	305
1983	298	352	362
1984	368	445	436
1985	308	141	143
1986	400	255	247
1987	667	461	200
1988	613	592	..

Sources: Index constructed from constant price data in *SIPRI Yearbook 1989: World Armaments and Disarmament* (Oxford University Press: Oxford, 1989), table 6A.2; Grimmelt, R., *CRS Report for Congress Trends in Conventional Arms Transfers to the Third World by Major Supplier, 1980–1988* (Library of Congress: Washington, DC, 1989); US Arms Control and Disarmament Agency, *World Military Expenditures and Arms Transfers 1988* (ACDA: Washington, DC, 1989).

(and even signed the Non-Proliferation Treaty after the sale). However, the threat and deterrence value remains in an area of great instability.

The three main sources of arms transfer data—SIPRI, the US Congressional Research Service (CRS), and the US Arms Control and Disarmament Agency (ACDA)—all show the volume of Chinese arms trade with the Third World as rising rapidly in the 1980s (see table 7.2). According to both SIPRI and CRS data, in 1988 China was the third largest arms exporter in the world, after the USSR and the USA. Since these sources give dollar values which are not comparable with each other, indices have been estimated for each series to denote trend indicators. All reveal essentially the same trend: a rapid rise during the decade. The SIPRI and CRS series shows a five- to sixfold increase (500–600 per cent) in 1981–88. The ACDA series shows a fourfold increase until 1984 and then a decline. By 1987, however, the volume of arms exports was still double that of 1981, according to ACDA data. By any reckoning these are phenomenal increases. Given that the Iraq–Iran War is officially over, yet arms purchases by the belligerents continue, although at a slower rate, it is not clear what the future of arms exports is for China. If commercialization continues, at the expense of ideological considerations, then exports may rise again after a lull.

It is almost impossible to know how much money China has actually made from arms sales. Certain transactions, say with Thailand, have been at 'friendship prices'. Others, clearly the Saudi ballistic missile sale, have earned a lot of foreign exchange. Annual sales of $1–2 billion have routinely been claimed from the mid-1980s. In 1989 the Chinese themselves claimed that in the previous year $260 million were earned from exports of the *aeronautics and astronautics industries alone*.[30] In addition, the defence establishment is earning foreign exchange through the sale of its civilian products— a direct spin-off of conversion. It is suggested here that, at a modest and conservative estimate, China has earned over $1 billion a year from sales by the defence industries. This could be worth about 4 billion yuan or about one-fifth of their announced military expenditure in 1988.

To sum up, China has reduced official military expenditure, releasing resources for the civilian economy. However, it has continued with incremental modernization of its forces at a slow but steady rate. In quantitative terms it probably has the third largest defence industry in the world, although qualitative comparisons will give it a far lower rank. The military part of the defence industrial base is being reduced through conversion. However, this allows the military to earn more from its own accounts and therefore mitigates the cut in budgetary funding. Essentially through earning profits, including substantial foreign arms sales, the PLA has preserved its modernization plans, consistent with the economic development of the country in general. Leaving aside the complex and moral issue of foreign arms sales, in other respects there is perhaps a lesson for other developing nations facing similar security environment.

III. Japan

During the 1980s Japan became an economic superpower. Its military capability also increased, and it is definitely a military regional power in an area of potential conflict. The political economy of security is particularly important for the country as it wrestles to reconcile the

---

[30] *Summary of World Broadcast Weekly*, 21 Feb. 1989, in IDSA (note 28).

often contradictory facets that characterize its foreign policy—both economic and political.

Japan contributes to international security, defined in the broadest sense, through both economic and military channels; however, it consistently stresses the former. Burden-sharing, particularly with the USA, encompasses many dimensions and ranges from providing more resources for US bases to providing more ODA to allies. Yet conflicts arise, particularly in trade and economic affairs, and these are bound to increase in the future. As the Soviet military threat recedes, non-military threats become more important. Japan's defence spending has increased rapidly in recent years; indeed, its defence growth rate was one of the highest in the world during the second half of the decade. On the other hand, its contribution to international economic security in the form of ODA also rose very fast, and in 1990 it is set to become the largest donor in the world, superseding the USA. More discussion on aid and security is to be found in chapter 9.

The 1 per cent limit

Discussions of Japanese military expenditures usually centre around the so-called 1 per cent limit.[31] This refers to the self-imposed ceiling set by the Cabinet in 1976 to limit defence spending to a maximum of 1 per cent of GNP. Although the upper bound has no status in law, it was until recently generally maintained by successive governments. In 1986 it was decided that, although the principle remains valid, the limit can be breached in practice; however, attempts would be made to keep within the norm. It was thought that the FY 1987 budget, of 3.517 trillion yen, would go above 1 per cent of the forecasted GNP. The Japanese defence White Paper, *Defense of Japan 1987*, predicting for the first time that the limit would be breached, claimed that the military burden would be 1.004 per cent of GNP.[32] However, actual expenditure was slightly lower, and GNP growth was higher than anticipated; hence the burden was of the order of 0.985 per cent.[33] Incidentally, it should be noted that SIPRI provides the ratio of defence spending as a share of GDP rather than GNP. The latter has

---

[31] See Tullberg, R. and Hagmeyer-Gaverus, G., 'World military expenditure', in SIPRI, *SIPRI Yearbook 1987: World Armaments and Disarmament* (Oxford University Press: Oxford, 1987), chapter 6.

[32] *Defense of Japan 1987* (Japan Defense Agency: Tokyo, 1987).

[33] *Japan Monitor*, June 1988, p. 7; details are from *Daily Yomiuri*, 17 June 1988.

been higher for Japan compared to the former. Hence the SIPRI estimates of military burden show that the 1 per cent limit may already had been exceeded even though, strictly in terms of the Japanese definition, this is not the case.

In a sense, concentrating attention on this limit obfuscates rather than clarifies the central issues surrounding Japanese defence expenditure, the country's military capability as well as the implications for regional and international security relations. A much more important indicator is the absolute amount of spending. In terms of current values, and the strong yen exchange-rate with respect to the US dollar, Japan is among the world's top military spenders; its rank is about sixth in the world. More significantly, the rate of increase in military expenditure has been high as the government strives to fulfil its current five-year defence plan. According to SIPRI estimates, the growth rate of defence spending in real terms in 1980–89 was about 4.3 per cent per annum, one of the highest for industrialized countries and far exceeding those of France, the FRG and the UK.

The Mid-Term Defense Plan, 1986–90, and military expenditure

The level of annual defence spending is determined by a forward planning process entitled the Mid-Term Defense Plan (MTDP) which provides estimated approximate targets of forces and assets for the Self Defense Forces (SDF). The current plan,[34] formulated in 1985, has allocated a sum of 18.5 trillion yen (in constant 1985 prices) for the five years beginning in FY 1986 and ending in FY 1990, with a planned annual growth rate of 5.4 per cent per year. Of the total for the five years, 41 per cent goes to personnel and provisions; 33 per cent for OM&S; and 26 per cent for weapon procurement. Each fiscal year budget should be implicitly related to the MTDP Estimate (*Chugyo*), but the relation is not exact.

By FY 1989, four years into the five-year plan, approximately 78 per cent of the aggregate expenditure had been completed. Therefore, plan fulfilment requires that the remaining 22 per cent would need to be spent in FY 1990. This implies a level of 4048 trillion yen (in 1985 prices) and represents the highest military expenditure in Japanese history.

---

[34] For details, see *Defense of Japan 1989* (Japan Defense Agency: Tokyo, 1989).

Table 7.3. Japan's defence budgets, FYs 1980–89

Year	Defence spending (b. yen)	Defence share in total budget (%)
1980	2 230.0	*5.2*
1981	2 400.0	*5.1*
1982	2 586.1	*5.2*
1983	2 754.2	*5.5*
1984	2 934.6	*5.8*
1985	3 137.1	*6.0*
1986	3 343.5	*6.2*
1987	3 517.4	*6.5*
1988	3 700.3	*6.5*
1989	3 919.8	*6.5*

Source: Defense of Japan 1989 (Japan Defense Agency: Tokyo, 1989).

Table 7.3 gives details of the defence budgets for the decade. The FY 1989 budget provides for about 3920 billion yuan, estimated to be 6.5 per cent of the budget and 1.006 per cent of GDP. The allocation scheme is somewhat different from NATO or US practice. The principal allocations in FY 1989 are the following: (*a*) personnel and provision: 1614 billion yuan, or 41.2 per cent of the total amount; (*b*) equipment and materials: 1098 billion yuan, 28 per cent; (*c*) maintenance: 594 billion yuan, 15.1 per cent; (*d*) expenses for bases: 374 billion yuan, 9.5 per cent; (*e*) facility expenses (construction): 113 billion yuan, 2.9 per cent; (*f*) R&D: 83 billion yuan, 2.1 per cent; and (*g*) others: 45 billion yuan, 1.2 per cent.

The allocation between investment and operating costs is approximately 60 : 40—a relatively high ratio, owing to the high amount expended on the bases. It is also interesting that R&D accounts for only 2 per cent; as a means of comparison, the United States and the Soviet Union spend 12 and 20 per cent of their defence budgets on military R&D, respectively. It is not surprising that the argument has been made that Japanese pre-eminence in civilian technology is possible because it is a modest investor in defence research. Alternatively, the declining economic and civilian technological competitiveness of the superpowers is due to their overwhelming emphasis on military R&D.

Table 7.4. Japan's major weapon stocks, 1989

Army	No.	Navy	No.	Air Force	No.
Tanks	1 190	Destroyers/ frigates	55	Fighters: F-15 F-4 F-1	120 125 74
Armoured vehicles	630	Submarines	14		
Field artillery	870	Anti-submarine patrol aircraft: P-3C P-23	50 29	Early-warning aircraft: E-2C	8
Anti-tank helicopters	40				

Source: Responsible Partner: Japan's Global Strategy (Embassy of Japan: Stockholm, 1989).

In terms of military capability, Japan seems to be making steady advances (see table 7.4 for details of major weapon systems currently held by the SDF). This is particularly true for its Naval Self Defense Forces, not surprising given its geographical position. Japan's naval force includes more than 50 major surface warships; the plans to equip two destroyers (constructed by domestic industry) with the Aegis shipborne air defence system (purchased from the USA) will further increase the naval capability. Recent rumours have suggested that Japan might be contemplating building its first aircraft-carrier, although this is still a politically sensitive issue domestically.

The catapulting of Japan into the topmost group of defence spenders has raised the nascent fear of militarization that bedevils South-East Asia and the Pacific region, given the unhappy experiences of the last world war. China has already openly voiced its concern, and other regional countries could be quietly apprehensive.[35] But one should always isolate military expenditure from militarization per se. The rapid growth of the former is neither a necessary nor sufficient condition for the existence of the latter. It is still early to predict that militarization is on the rise in Japan.

[35] *Defence Monitor*, 3 Feb. 1988, p. 6040.

In spite of the high growth rate of real (inflation-adjusted) military expenditure (see appendix A, table A3), there is much other evidence that 'pacifism' and self-defence, rather than aggression, are the central motivating forces behind Japan's international security relations. It steadfastly refuses to participate in security assistance programmes and overseas military activities; witness the unwillingness to police the Gulf even though its economic life depends on oil flows. Until recently the country was not even a member of the UN peace-keeping forces; its first contribution of military personnel was for Afghanistan.[36]

Japan has also shown, through its actions, that military and economic security cannot be delinked. It compensates for its lack of foreign military involvement and help by providing large quantities of economic and humanitarian aid. It is currently the second largest aid donor in the world and in the next decade will outstrip the USA as the world's foremost donor. The Cabinet has approved a plan whereby official development assistance could rise to $50 billion during 1988–92; this is double the amount being spent in the period 1983–88. In addition, the 1988 Toronto summit meeting of the leading industrialized nations of the world (the Group of Seven, or G7) saw the most innovative proposal on debt reductions and forgiveness for the poorest countries in the developing world coming from Prime Minister Takeshita.[37]

Japan is an industrial giant, but its arms production is an insignificant portion of total manufacturing output; in 1987 (the latest year for which data are available) weapon output was only 0.06 per cent of total industrial production. Even large corporations, dependent on defence contracts, are generally unenthusiastic. One reason is that arms exports are negligible and the domestic market is not capable of providing sufficient profits. Also, companies like Mitsubishi Heavy Industries (MHI, the largest defence contractor) and Kawasaki Heavy Industries (KHI, the second largest), which are heavily involved in weapon production, are also industrial giants in their respective civilian fields. Exposure to the arms market is generally low: MHI

---

[36] For an analysis, see *Japan Monitor*, Nov. 1988, p. 14, report from *Daily Yomiuri*, 13 Nov. 1988.
[37] *Financial Times*, 30 Sep. 1988, p. 18.

gets only 15 per cent of its total sales from the military; KHI has a corresponding ratio of 30 per cent, and this seems to be the highest.[38]

Japanese industry is interested in armaments but only as means to diversification, spreading of risks, since defence ministry orders are less dictated by market fluctuations, as well as gaining the fruits of technological spin-off. Given the small size of the market, and the almost impossibility of exports under current practice, it is difficult to see overwhelming interest by industry in this fields. It is true that 'Japan has the technological and industrial capability to become a great military power quickly'[39] particularly through the exploitation of dual-use technology. However, the possibility is remote as yet.

The Japanese Government stresses domestic procurement. In 1987 (the latest year for which data are available), domestic purchases amounted to 91 per cent of total equipment purchase. According to the White Paper, in 1986 arms imports from commercial purchases and those through the US Foreign Military Sales (FMS) programme came to only 146 billion yuan, slightly over $1 billion.[40] Yet US sources have claimed that arms imports exceed $2 billion annually. The discrepancy between the two could be due to the value of technology transfers to local companies, which Japanese defence sources may have subsumed under 'domestic procurement'. According to SIPRI data, Japan is the industrial world's largest importer of major weapons (including licensed technology). Almost all imports come from the USA.

The security of Japan and relations with the USA

US Japanese security relations in all aspects—military, economic and political—are getting more complicated. Three particular issues, surfacing at the end of the 1980s, exemplify the complexities: technology transfer and co-operation in the FS-X fighter case; burden-sharing for US bases; and trade conflicts.

In 1985 the Air Self Defense Forces began the discussion of the replacement for the F-1 support fighter. The development of the new-

---

[38] See *Far Eastern Economic Review*, 13 Oct. 1988, for a discussion on defence industrialization in Japan. The article also analyses the reasons for Japan not exporting any arms (although it has the industrial power to do so); hence, profitability remains low.

[39] Report of Western European Union, *Outlook for Future Development in the Japanese Armaments Industry and its Possible Repercussions on Europe* (WEU: Paris, Sep. 1985).

[40] See note 34.

generation aircraft, termed the Fighter Support Experimental (FS-X), was an important test of Japanese technology. Although initially there was a consensus for domestic development and indigenous technology, by 1987 co-development of the General Dynamics F-16 or the McDonnell Douglas F-18 was accepted as the preferred mode of operation. In November 1988 a Memorandum of Understanding (MOU) was signed by the two countries; early the next year Mitsubishi (the prime contractor) and General Dynamics finalized agreement for the joint development of the FS-X based on substantial improvements to the F-16. Japan would bear the entire cost and its industry would receive about 60 per cent of industrial work on the project.

The deal was considered, by the Japanese, to be extremely favourable to the Americans. It was also hailed as a model for future industrial co-operation particularly in dual-capable civil–military technologies. However, resentment spread rapidly in Japan as the US Congress 'reopened' the case in 1989, with President Bush in power. Production shares, sensitive technology transfers, the relation between defence and trade issues as well as the 'giving away' of aeronautic technology to a rival power were all contentious issues raised in a controversial debate.

Although the difficulties are now sorted out and development has begun, the whole chequered history of the project shows the problems that US–Japanese relations may encounter. A respected local research institute puts it succinctly: 'The experience with the FS-X, which was intended to to be a model for future joint weapons development projects, has served more to reveal the difficulties of such cooperation than its usefulness. What was expected to be a first step on the joint production road may prove instead to be the last for some time to come'.[41]

In this context it should be stressed that the burden-sharing debate has also been extended to Japan with considerable discussion, in US circles, as to how the Japanese can best contribute to their own security effort. According to the USA, three key functions, in terms of self-reliant military effort, need to be fulfilled: protection of the Japanese archipelago from invasion *without* US assistance; protection of the sea lanes of communication (SLOC) up to 1000 nautical miles; and finally, the closing of the straits, during war, to hinder the Soviet

[41] *Asian Security 1989–1990* (Brassey's: London, 1989), p. 72.

fleet from moving out into the Pacific Ocean. The House Burden-sharing Panel was sceptical about the willingness or the ability of Japan to perform these functions.

As regards the economics of burden-sharing, the Japanese claim to spend almost 10 per cent of their defence budget on US bases; the total is approaching $3 billion.[42] According to domestic sources, the expenditure per US serviceman is of the order of $45 000; however, this number is strongly contested by congressional sources[43] which claim that it includes 'non-outlays' such as estimates of rental and user cost of land supplied free to the USA. The debate on burden-sharing usually considers a narrow measure, that of expenditure on the US bases in Japan. These have been increasing rapidly in recent years, usually faster than the aggregate spending on the military. However, the central issue is the wider measure of the security burden. As mentioned above, the non-military aspects of security are important determinants of Japanese strategic perceptions; here their contribution is high and significant.

The trade imbalance between Japan and the USA is a continuing irritant and could become a security issue. As the US trade deficit has grown (see chapter 5) so also has the pressure increased on Japan to liberalize its trading regime and allow more US goods. The Omnibus Trade and Competitiveness Act allows the US Government to list 'priority' countries which condone practices 'including major barriers and trade distorting practices, the elimination of which are likely to have the most significant potential to increase United States exports'.[44] The naming of such priority countries is an indication of which are considered to be in 'trade conflict' with the USA owing to their unfair trade practices. The relevant section 301 is often called the 'Super 310'; in 1989 Bush named the first three countries under this law as Japan, Brazil and India. This has created a large amount of ill feeling all round. The rapid rise of foreign investment by Japanese companies in US business is another cause for Washington's concern; the level of such investment (transfer of US wealth into Japanese hands) doubled in 1984–87. Currently, the round of talks under the Structural Impediments Initiative (SII) is being conducted to sort out these deep-rooted structural problems in bilateral relationships.

---

[42] See note 32.
[43] *Report of the Defense Burdensharing Panel of the Committee on Armed Services, US House of Representatives* (US Government Printing Office: Washington, DC, Aug. 1988).
[44] See note 41.

In a sense Japanese security relations with the rest of the world are a curious mixture of ambivalent and at times contradictory attitudes.

1. There is a conceptual issue of what exactly 'security' means and how military and non-military factors should interact. The Japanese believe that their economic might may be an useful *substitute* for military power, towards global stability, provided the USA buttresses them militarily. US congressional statements are divided; they range from urging Japan to drop their self-imposed limit on the defence burden (and spend much more on the military) to targeting increased economic aid to Western allies. But it is difficult to see how both can be feasible.

2. There could be a contradiction between domestic and foreign points of view. The politicization of foreign aid is one case in question. ODA policy has been based on economic self-interest and humanitarian concerns. Helping US allies in the Middle East or giving much more aid to the Philippines does not necessarily fit squarely with their philosophy; yet that is what the USA wants.

3. The direct relations with the USA in all its multifarious aspects (defence capability, technology transfers, expenditure on bases, trade relations, protectionism and liberalization, role as a regional and international power, common attitudes and divergent cultural perceptions) are becoming increasingly complex. There are now vociferous revisionist analysts in the USA who would like to have a go at 'Japan-bashing'. Similar Japanese responses, as yet muted, can only increase. In 1989 Shintaro Ishihara, a member of the Diet, and Sony Chairman, Akio Morita, published a book entitled *'No' to ieru Nihon [The Japan That Can Say 'NO']*:[45] this may be the beginning of a protracted war of words which yet underline a fundamental divergence in national views.

Finally, there is the potential for controversy between US interests and those of the nations in the region. The former would like Japanese military capability for self-defence to rise; the latter are tense about Japanese militarism and its allegedly threatening implications. How these can be squared is yet to be seen.

---

[45] Ishihara, S., and Morita, A., *'No' to ieru Nihon [The Japan That Can Say 'No']* (Kobunsha: Tokyo, 1989).

IV. The two Korean states

The complex web of military, strategic, political, social and economic factors that constitute security are nowhere more evident in Asia than in the two Korean states. Within recent history, four major powers—the USA, the USSR, China and Japan—have been militarily involved in the Korean peninsula. The division of Korea is still unacceptable to the people, even though geo-political reality dictates that it must continue in the foreseeable future.

More important than the geographical division is the ideological gulf that separates the countries. North Korea, ruled by an authoritarian regime, had a strong economy in the past (but which seems to have lost its dynamism), has high military expenditures (relative to its national product), pursues an inward-looking strategy of development and preserves a tightrope neutrality with its two biggest supporters—the USSR and China. South Korea has recently emerged from its own authoritarian rule and is trying to evolve as a young democracy. Student and labour unrest, caused by demands for greater freedom and less repressive labour laws, creates difficulties for internal security. With high growth rates, an outward-looking economic strategy, a dynamic export sector and rising real income, the health of the economy is assured. Military expenditure and the defence burden are high and growing. Relations with the USA, its principal ally, are a curious mixture of co-operation and confrontation. Military relations are cordial but economic (trade) relations remain a bone of contention.

Much more so than any other country in the region, the two Koreas come closest to a European 'model' of security perception.[46] More specifically, it looks relatively similar to the two German states and their recent historical experience. The existence of a clearly demarcated dividing line between the opposite blocs; the distrust arising from division coupled with the unfulfilled dreams of unification; the presence of military forces with clearly defined functions under an integrated command; foreign troops and their basing facilities creating a bone of contention at various levels; and irritation with the main allies at the entwined nature of security with economic factors, such as trade imbalance or foreign aid, causing

[46] See Kissinger, H., 'East Asia, the Pacific and the West: strategic trends and implication', in *East Asia, the West and International Security: Prospects for Peace*, Adelphi Papers 216 (International Institute for Strategic Studies: London, 1987).

frictions—these are all familiar features in the European context yet uncommon in the region under discussion.

The successful holding of the 1988 Olympic Games, although of symbolic significance, has catapulted South Korea into the ranks of the major countries of the world. There is now talk of gaining admittance to the OECD, the rich nations' club. But after the glitter, worries remain about domestic political stability. President Roh Tae Woo's unexpected victory in the first direct presidential contest, after 16 years, in December 1987 was followed by the failure of his party to secure a majority in Parliament in the nation-wide elections of April 1988. The government faces student unrest, demands for more openness in the political process, demands for greater dialogue with the North, and attempts by organized labour to improve its economic position after decades of repression and failure to increase wages compatible with the country's phenomenal growth. Part of the South Korean 'miracle' can be attributed to low labour costs. There are two reasons for this: labour has been willing to accept austerity wages so long as economic development was limited and the bogey of foreign involvement (from the North) accepted as a real threat; and successive military and non-democratic regimes used strong arm policies to keep wage demands low. None of these conditions are thought to hold any more. How the rapid growth of the economy will be sustained as costs rise is a matter for further analysis.

South Korea's relations with the USA are increasingly fraught with difficulties. 1988 saw relatively violent student demonstrations and other signs of anti-Americanism. This was linked with strident calls during the year for re-unification with the North. There was also some inconclusive discussion about whether there should be a change to the system whereby a US officer heads the Combined Forces Command and has operational control over the Korean forces. Overall, however, military relations at the governmental levels are cordial since there is a clear understanding of the mutual beneficial advantages for both countries. South Korea's defence burden is high. Yet the new cost-sharing rules, agreed to at the end of the decade, increased the Korean contribution to the combined defence projects (infrastructural programmes) from $34 million to $40 million from 1989.

In early 1990, a US Department of Defense report announced force reductions in the region within the context of a three-phase plan. In the first phase, 1990–92, about 15 000 US forces of the 135 000 currently deployed (about 11 per cent) would be cut. These forward-deployed personnel in Asia are mainly spread over the bases in Japan, the Philippines and South Korea. For South Korea itself, the core combat forces in the form of the 2nd Infantry Division will remain intact; the reduction of 7000 personnel, out of a total of 44 000, is expected to come mainly from administrative staff. Details of the second and third phases (running from 1993 to the mid-1990s and then until 2000) are yet to be specified and will depend on the security environment prevalent then. According to this report,[47] host-nation support provided by South Korea amounts to 13 per cent of total costs for US forces deployed in the country. An alternative estimate[48] claims that the host government provides about $1.91 billion for the basing facilities, while the USA spends about $3 billion there. It is felt by both governments that the burden-sharing remains equitable.[49]

The real controversy, which is bound to become more fierce with time, relates to trade and the allegedly 'unfair' advantages that the low-cost economies possess. Although there is little backing in economic theory or political judgement regarding the US position, it is clear that populist pressures will dictate a hardening of positions. South Korea's trade surplus with the USA is around $ 10 billion; on the other hand, about 20 per cent of aggregate trade deficit of the USA is with the Asian NICs. The USA has threatened to remove Korea from the countries eligible for tariff exemptions under the Generalized System of Preferences; this will hurt exports, which will be subject to controls. There is growing pressure to increase the value of the currency, the won, with respect to the US dollar so that US goods can become cheaper. There is also arm-twisting about opening up domestic markets in Korea and allowing in more US goods without protectionism.

As Korea 'does another Japan' and becomes economically strong, but still requiring the military help of the superpower ally to counter the alleged threat from the North, bilateral relations will tend to be problematic. This cannot but create resentment and domestic political repercussions. The best option for the government, within the general framework of international *détente*, would be to patch up relations with its neighbour. There are some signs that North Korea is serious about its declared intention to normalize relations. In 1987 it

[47] *Far Eastern Economic Review*, vol. 148, no. 18 (3 May 1990), pp. 10–11.
[48] *Asian Security 1988–89* (note 18).
[49] See note 48.

announced a unilateral force reduction of 100 000 men as a gesture of confidence building; by the beginning of 1988 this was completed. It has also made proposals for creating a zone of peace in the demilitarized zone dividing the country and sundry other measures for mutual disarmament. The catch, from the South's point of view, is the demand for the removal of US bases, which is not acceptable.

Although North Korea has made significant strides in industrialization, its overall economic performance is weaker. Until the mid-1970s the North probably had a slightly higher per capita income; but it grew very slowly afterwards, while the South achieved its economic 'miracle'. Today, North Korea has an average income which is possibly half that of its neighbour; with a population which is also half as large, the total GDP is probably only a quarter of South Korea's. With a much lower national income, and military expenditures at similar levels, the defence burden is much higher. Therefore, it cannot afford to spend as much as it does, given the weak economic base and the adverse effects of the re-allocation of resources. On the other hand, South Korea's military expenditure now exceeds $8 billion (see appendix A, table A3), and it has grown in real terms by 5.6 per cent over the 1980s. Its defence growth has been the fastest in South-East Asia, but because of economic growth as much as threat perception. Estimates of capabilities and force structures tend to show that North Korea may be slightly superior to the South, although the latter is catching up fast. According to a local analyst, the former started its arms buildup in 1964, while the latter followed 12 years later; hence there has been an asymmetric arms race.[50]

Both countries are significant arms producers by Third World standards. For South Korea this was necessary after the soul-searching consequent to US withdrawal from Viet Nam and the desire for more self-sufficiency from its superpower ally. In addition, it could build on its rapidly expanding industrial base. In shipbuilding, for example, Hyundai Shipbuilding and Heavy Industries moved into the construction of fighting ships, utilizing its expertise in the civilian sector. South Korea also produces fighters (Northrop F-5), aircraft engines and fuselage (for the F-16), tanks (including the indigenous '88 Tank) as well as a variety of missiles. Arms exports also increased rapidly in the 1980s, but they have slowed down in recent years,

---

[50] Chongwhi, K., 'The security of East Asia', in *East Asia, the West and International Security: Prospects for Peace*, Adelphi Papers 218 (International Institute for Strategic Studies: London, 1987).

allegedly because of US pressures on third-country sale of joint technology. However, problems have multiplied; capacity utilization remains low; profits are smaller than in the civilian sectors; and the economic rationale for having a domestic industry is not easy to find, even though military security interests decree otherwise. For North Korea, domestic production of weapons is a part of an overall economic philosophy which stresses self-reliant development. But, given the limited nature of the domestic markets and the difficulties of small production runs, both countries have turned to export markets; the North has been much more active, given its greater need for foreign exchange and isolation from the world community. In spite of domestic production, however, major force modernizations are dependent on foreign arms, and both the Soviet Union and the United States have been large-scale suppliers. The South, in addition, enjoys a nuclear deterrent protection which the other country does not have.

8. The Third World: conflict resolution

I. Conflicts and wars

The 1980s have seen an unusually high degree of conflict, which has caused a number of major wars in the Third World. Throughout the decade, wars characterized nearly every single region in the developing world: Argentina (with the UK) in Latin America; Nicaragua and El Salvador in Central America; wars in numerous places on the continent of Africa, particularly in the Horn and Southern Africa; the Afghanistan conflict, well known for the first long-term direct involvement of a superpower after Viet Nam, in South Asia; unabated conflict in Indo-China, particularly in Cambodia, in the Far East; and of course the Iraq–Iran War in the Middle East, the bloodiest conflagration of the period.

By the end of the decade, war fatigue, national inertia and financial costs had all contributed to the cessation of direct hostilities in many of these cases, and conflict resolution now seems to be the norm rather than the exception. Argentina saw the ousting of its military dictatorship and a return of democracy; the dignified change of the Sandinista Government through democratic elections in Nicaragua and the disinvolvement of the USA in support of the Contras raised hopes for a long-lasting regional peace settlement; the independence of Namibia and the announcement of the progressive withdrawal of South African troops from neighbouring states were positive signs of a reduction in the malignant influence of the apartheid regime; Soviet troop withdrawal from Afghanistan and Vietnamese troop withdrawal from Cambodia raised the prospect of peace in Asia; and finally, in the Middle East, the Iraq–Iran War ended in a stalemate.

According to data published by SIPRI, the number of major Third World conflicts has been declining since about 1986.[1] However, the decline has been painfully slow, and the potential for escalation remains strong. For the Third World as a whole, in 1989 the number

[1] See *SIPRI Yearbooks 1987, 1988, 1989* and *1990: World Armaments and Disarmament* (Oxford University Press: Oxford, 1987, 1988, 1989 and 1990), chapters 8, 9, 9 and 10, respectively.

of major conflicts was 30; this was fewer than the 35 conflicts recorded for 1986 and 1987 and the 34 recorded for 1988. If the USA–Panama war is considered exceptional, major conflicts in the developing countries fell from 35 to 29 from 1986 to 1989. Although this is still a large number of conflicts, the numbers for the period represent a downward trend.[2]

Yet, the potential for major inter-state conflicts remains dormant and could be incited quickly. In 1990, for example, India and Pakistan are conducting foreign policy brinkmanship over the Kashmir separatism issue which could still produce a major war reminiscent of the last one, in 1971. The Middle East remains an overarmed and dangerous region, with numerous unsolved issues ranging from deterrence through NCB (nuclear, biological and chemical) weapons to political support for the *intifada* movement in Palestine.

A central feature of Third World conflicts is the preponderance of intra-state wars as opposed to the canonical concept of international relations, where the state had a monopoly on legitimate violence within its borders and conflict was essentially an inter-state phenomenon. Indeed, this feature has been labelled as the co-existence of 'inter-state "comity" and intra-state "anarchy"'.[3] Data produced by the Department of Peace and Conflict Research of Uppsala University on all conflicts, major and minor, clearly indicate this pattern.[4] A threefold classification is made: classic wars between two governments utilizing military forces; wars of state formation involving the government and an opposition group asking for autonomy or separation; and internal wars where the predominant motive is the domestic change of government. These can be reinterpreted as: classic inter-state conflicts; denial of the legitimacy of the state; and denial of the legitimacy of the government. Of the 111 conflicts recorded for 1988, the first category contained 12 conflicts (11 per cent of the total), the second category 36 conflicts (32 per cent), and the third group 63 conflicts (57 per cent). Clearly, the classical viewpoint of inter-state wars, the so-called 'external'

---

[2] These figures are adjusted from basic data given in Lindgren, K., Wilson, G. K., Wallensteen, P. and Nordquist, K-A., 'Major armed conflicts in 1989', *SIPRI Yearbook 1990* (note 1), chapter 10. See also Wallensteen, P. (ed.), *States in Armed Conflict 1988*, Report no. 30 (Department of Peace and Conflict Research, Uppsala University: Uppsala, Sweden, July 1989), particularly the paper by Alker, H. R., 'Uppsala fireworks: data-based thoughts on the origins and possible obsolescence of the European state system'.
[3] Alker in Wallensteen (note 2), p. 22.
[4] Wallensteen (note 2).

conflicts, have less relevance for today's Third World. The major source of problems stems from 'internal' factors. These can range from developmental failures to inefficient functioning of government. Outside influence and intervention then act as a catalyst to increase tension and often produce an open war rather than a continuing covert conflict.

One of the major causes of high military expenditure, for any country, is the existence of conflict and wars, particularly when related to an arms race with neighbours. As discussed in chapter 1, Third World military expenditures are highly concentrated, with the major proportion expended by a relatively few countries. Leaving out China, which has a world power status, total Third World military expenditure was approximately $130 billion in 1988. Seven countries alone—Egypt, India, Iran, Iraq, Israel, South Korea and Taiwan— spent around $50 billion, or over 40 per cent of the total. All of these countries identify major inter-sate conflicts as the principal rationale for excessively high defence spending.

The same trend, of high levels and concentration, is evident for the trade in arms.[5] In 1985–89, 10 countries alone imported over two-thirds of the whole Third World's major weapon imports. These were India, Iraq, Saudi Arabia, Syria, Egypt, North Korea, Afghanistan, Angola, Libya and Taiwan. Except for the oil-rich countries of Saudi Arabia and Libya, all of the others claim major international disputes and conflicts with neighbours. Modern wars are inherently costly. If the loss of economic assets and potential are added to these military costs, then the total financial expenditures rapidly become excessive for poor developing countries.

The Iraq–Iran War

The end of the eight-year Iraq–Iran War was signalled in July 1988 by the acceptance, by Iran, of UN resolution 598 for a cease-fire; Iraq had previously accepted the resolution, although it showed some reluctance to go along with the implications of the resolution at the time when its adversary accepted it. The peace negotiations, conducted in

[5] Deger, S., 'Recent patterns of arms trade and regional conflict', paper prepared for the 39th Annual Pugwash Conference, Cambridge, Mass., July 1989, which documents the interrelationships between concentration and conflict in the Third World arms transfer process. See also Anthony, I., 'The trade in major conventional weapons', *SIPRI Yearbook 1989* (note 1), chapter 6; and Anthony, I. and Wulf, H., 'The trade in major conventional weapons', *SIPRI Yearbook 1990* (note 1), chapter 7.

Geneva under UN auspices, have not been smooth, but there are hopes that after the costly and bloody conflict both sides are interested in some form of peace, although still retaining their adversarial positions in international relations. Both military expenditure and arms imports have declined in 1989, compared to previous years, but whether this 'inertia' brought on by the unprecedented cost of the war will continue or not is difficult to forecast.

Various causes and competing hypotheses have been put forward regarding the origins of the war. It has been variously attributed to personal animosity between Ayatollah Khomeini and President Saddam Hussein, to the historical socio-cultural feud between the Persians and the Arabs, to the schism in Islam between Shi'ites and Sunnis, to the arms race nourished by the oil wealth as well as to desires for regional hegemonic dominance. All of these explanations are partial, although each does help to explain a part of this multi-faceted problem.

The military lessons of this war, for Third World countries, may be significant, and analysts need to ponder on this complex issue. One salient feature seems to be the primacy of defensive over offensive strategies. Almost all the major offensive 'breakthroughs' seemed to get bogged down after successful beginnings.[6] For both countries, a see-saw progression ended in a series of stalemates. The adversaries used different strategies forced upon them by overall constraints. Iran, unable to import the amount of arms it needed, adopted a labour-intensive war-fighting technology, essentially a modified version of the human wave. It was helped by the morale of its people and forces, particularly the para-military volunteers such as the Basij and the Pasardan. Iraq, in a much more favourable position in terms of arms imports, preferred more modern equipment and weapons. Its leaders were also hampered by fears of domestic revolt and dissatisfaction as the burdens of the war grew; hence, human losses were sought to be minimized.

Whichever way one looks at it, this war was expensive and the costs were excessive, even for two of the richest Third World nations. No analysis of human, social and economic costs can be accurate, given the prolonged nature, secrecy, difficulties of verification and economic disruption of the armed conflict. Estimates suggest half a million casualities in the armed forces, huge numbers of civilian

---

[6] Chubin, S. and Tripp, C., *Iran and Iraq at War* (Tauris: London, 1988), chapter 4.

deaths, and almost one and a half million refugees from the war zone. There are no figures for the number of war veterans or those crippled by this war. The opportunity costs of the war, that is, the amount of investment, consumption and economic growth that would have been possible in its absence, are exceedingly high. The Speaker of the Iranian Majlis, Hashemi Rafsanjani, indicated this clearly in 1985: 'If we had spent the budget allocation of four and a half years of the imposed war, that is 4000 to 5000 billion rials [$43.4–$54.3 billion] on industry, today we would be one of the most powerful countries in the world'.[7]

Five sets of financial and economic costs were incurred by the belligerents in this war: (a) military expenditure to pay for the war, particularly in terms of personnel and O&M; (b) arms imports, part of which are accounted by defence spending but a substantial part from extra-budgetary accounts and special foreign exchange allocations; (c) loss to national wealth and war damages, particularly in the oil sector; (d) costs of compensating the war dead ('martyrs'), veterans, pensions and refugees from the war zone, the so-called human costs; and (e) the opportunity costs of the war, in terms of lost output, investment and future growth.

SIPRI estimates show that the belligerents together may have spent $170–$200 billion on military activities, excluding arms imports. These are financial costs associated with the domestic military input to the war effort, but they leave out war damages as well as human costs. The information sheet prepared by SIPRI in August 1988 provides more detailed data on the breakdown of the above numbers.[8] SIPRI arms imports data are trend-indicator values and should not be added to the defence spending figures. ACDA data, which are closer to financial costs, show that the two countries could have imported over $50 billion worth of weapons in 1980–87.[9]

The extent of war damage is as yet difficult to calculate. Some 'guesstimates' state figures such as $500 billion as the amount that the two countries need in order to rebuild their infrastructure and productive systems. Losses in productive facilities in the oil sector were probably less than feared since the combatants avoided crippling each

---

[7] See note 6, p. 128.
[8] 'The Iraq–Iran War 1980–1988: military costs and arms transfers', SIPRI Information Sheet, Aug. 1988 (available on request from SIPRI).
[9] US Arms Control and Disarmament Agency, *World Military Expenditure and Arms Transfers 1988* (US Government Printing Office: Washington, DC, 1989).

other's principal source of revenue for the war. However, the absolute numbers are high. The Iranian Government claimed damages worth $160 billion up to 1985[10] in the oil industry alone. Therefore, the total war period losses in the oil sector alone could be around $250 billion. Information from Iraq is much more scarce, but there is no reason to suppose that the situation there was very different.

The governments have also had to compensate the families of the dead. For Iran, this is a sacred obligation since the deceased are considered *Shaheeds* (martyrs) in a holy war; but for Iraq, domestic dissatisfaction would also have been unbearable if compensation was not high. Again, Iranian data are more forthcoming; the families received 2 million rials (about $30 000) each which, considering the large numbers of war dead, could rise to a total sum in excess of $1 billion for families of the Iranian war dead.

An indication of the costs for Iraq is the extent of its international indebtedness, where it is now one of the largest debtors, having started the war as one of the richest nations in the Third World. In 1977, much before the second oil price rise of 1979 which improved its financial position at the start of the war in 1980, Iraq had foreign reserves of around $6.7 billion. Today it has foreign debts of at least 10 times as much; some estimates put it at $75 billion.[11]

To put the cost figures in perspective, they can be compared to the oil revenues that Iran and Iraq consider as their economic life-blood. Estimates show that the total historic earnings from oil for both countries taken together, from the first oil exports in 1919 for Iran and 1931 for Iraq until the end of the war, would be worth around $400 billion.[12] If the total cost of the war, including military expenditures, war damage, other payments and arms imports, are all added up, there is no doubt that it exceeds all the oil revenue that the combatants have ever earned.

---

[10] For various claims made by the Iranian Government, see *Summary Report: An Estimate of the Economic Damages of the Imposed War of Iraq against Iran* (Islamic Republic of Iran, Plan and Budget Organization: Tehran, 1983); McLachlen, K. and Joffe, G., *The Gulf War: A Survey of Political Issues and Economic Consequences* (Economist Intelligence Unit: London, 1984); and note 6. These claims must be treated with caution since they could have been formulated to claim reparation payments. However, more conservative estimates by the present authors show that orders of magnitude are not essentially different.

[11] For various estimates of the debt burden and depletion of Iraqi reserves, see *International Herald Tribune*, 4 Aug. 1988; International Monetary Fund, *International Financial Statistics*, various issues; and International Institute for Strategic Studies, *The Military Balance 1988–1989* (IISS: London, 1988).

[12] Authors' estimates.

It is difficult to predict defence spending trends for the future, given the volatility of the countries concerned, but the massive costs of the war suggest that domestic military expenditure will probably fall sharply in real terms, even though arms imports may rise as the erstwhile combatants try to replenish their inventories. One disturbing off-shoot of the war has been the increase in domestic arms production, particularly by Iran. Officials have claimed that Iran produces 70–80 per cent of all its ammunition needs; it is self-sufficient in bullets and mortar shells, produces anti-tank missiles, and is on its way to manufacturing sophisticated missile technology in the forms of SAMs and (Scud) SSMs.[13] This would enhance the capabilities of the combatants to fight limited but long-drawn-out wars of attrition without worrying about embargoes.

The Afghanistan–USSR War

The beginning of the Soviet troop withdrawal from Afghanistan marked the end of a phase in that wretched country's recent history but probably failed to bring true peace very much nearer. Soviet forces started moving out in May 1988 but by August the withdrawal was temporarily halted.[14] However, by the deadline of 15 February 1989, all foreign troops had left the country. Both the Majibullah regime and the various Mujahideen groups are committed to keeping the conflict going, aided and abetted by the superpowers' arms supplies. The war therefore continues. The country, one of the most impoverished in the world, is now in ruin. Over 1 million people are reported to have died. There are about 5 million refugees in Pakistan and Iran, and few have returned as yet. Per capita income for 1986 is estimated to have been around $166.[15] This places Afghanistan among the eight poorest countries in the world. The socio-economic situation is obviously much worse than in the case of Iran or Iraq since the government has neither the means nor the ability to provide help to its people.

Primary open sources have failed to provide any reasonably reliable data on Afghan military expenditure. SIPRI does not publish budgetary data since it is difficult to ascertain the extent of defence-

[13] See note 6.

[14] See *Financial Times*, 5 Nov. 1988 and 12 Nov. 1988; and *The Economist*, 7 Jan. 1989, p. 18.

[15] Calculated from basic data given in *The Europa Yearbook* (Europa Publications: London, 1988).

related spending. However, Soviet foreign aid must have been a major determinant of military expenditure and weapon procurement. Hence the actual government budgetary allocations could have been commensurately low relative to the intensity of the war.

The same level of secrecy has surrounded information on the costs of the Afghanistan War. Soviet military spending for this war is now known to be 45 billion roubles, or around $75 billion at official exchange-rates. US military supplies to the Mujahideen, financed by Saudi Arabia and channelled through Pakistan, have been substantial. Adding the personnel costs of the Afghan Army, a preliminary estimate of the total cost of the Afghanistan War can be made—around $100 billion. The total is astoundingly high, particularly if compared to the socio-economic needs of one of the poorest regions in the world.

II. Arms control and conflict resolution

The recent success of arms control negotiations between the major powers has raised questions as to why Third World regional arms control is conspicuous by its absence. It is of course worth noting that the history of European arms control is rather chequered; it is only very recently that the speed has accelerated. The Mutual and Balanced Force Reduction (MBFR) Talks continued for over a decade without any tangible results. Further, unilateral reductions by the USSR and structural disarmament in the West have had more impact on cuts in arms assets (as discussed in chapter 2) than any proposals emanating from the CFE Negotiation as yet. In addition, current reductions are starting from very high levels of weapon stocks, and some of the cuts are made for the sake of obsolescence and the needs of modernization. Nevertheless, there is little doubt that arms control has had tangible successes in recent years within the East–West framework.

Political change, particularly in the Soviet leadership, has motivated and acted as a catalyst for arms control in Europe. The same degree of vision is as yet lacking elsewhere. More important are fundamental factors in the Third World which preclude even confidence- and security-building measures which could be the first step towards greater control over the growth of arms. There have been many more 'hot' wars in the Third World. These are aptly named the 'Third World wars', and such open conflicts produce enduring insecurity.

The absence of orderly arrangements within the bloc system, with identifiable alliances facing each other, creates problems of managing arms control. The presence of a multipolar structure, where it is difficult to identify clear-cut 'friends' and 'enemies', as in the Asia–Pacific region discussed in chapter 7, also creates problems for the negotiations. The lack of institutions, such as the CSCE, hinders the process. Since many conflicts are related to questioning the legitimacy of the government or the state, it is not always clear as to which authority has the required mandate for negotiations. Finally, the intertwined nature of security, with military, political and economic aspects all linked together, makes it difficult to come to agreement about 'single issue' discussions.

Where arms control has been even marginally successful, such as in reducing the growth of arms acquisition and the cessation of conflicts, it has been for structural reasons rather than the political will of the participants. A central structural reason for conflict resolution has been the prohibitive cost of war and the increasingly expensive task of acquiring imported foreign arms to fight modern wars. As mentioned above, the Iraq–Iran War cost the two countries more than all their oil revenues ever earned, and the combatants in Afghanistan spent around $100 billion in their war. The Falklands/Malvinas War raised Argentina's defence burden to over 7 per cent, the highest in its modern history. Clearly, few governments and societies can afford to continue with protracted wars.

It is now time for Third World governments to appreciate that more positive steps need to be taken to resolve outstanding disputes through the orderly process of confidence-building measures and arms control negotiations. Economic difficulties could be used an an opportunity to facilitate weapon reductions. Given the negative relationship between defence spending and economic growth, arms control may set up a virtuous cycle implicit in the arguments for disarmament and development. Sir Brian Urquhart has aptly claimed that:

prolonged regional wars with no forseeable conclusive military outcome have become a costly proposition for all concerned. They are particularly devastating to the economies of Third World countries in conflict areas, where manpower and budget allocations for defence takes priority over social and economic development. Unilateral involvement of either of the superpowers in such regional conflicts has also proved to be politically and financially expensive for the superpowers as well as exacerbating the regional conflict itself.[16]

With the new *détente*, and the increasingly effective role of the United Nations, conflict resolution must be emphasized more and more. However, if the seeds of conflict inherent in developmental failures are always present, it will be difficult to preserve stability. Chapter 9 identifies these elements of economic security.

A lesson from the experience of Europe may be learned by countries involved in regional conflicts, say, in South Asia or the Asia–Pacific region. There is a strong need for institutional structures, similar to the CSCE, in Third World conflict resolution negotiations. The present authors have proposed elsewhere[17] the type of institutional framework that a Conference on Security and Co-operation in Asia (a so-called CSCA) should have. Simple confidence-building measures—such as more transparency in revealing details of military expenditures, notifying exercises by the armed forces, particularly in sensitive border areas, and linking economies through more bilateral contacts—will be helpful to start with. In the long run arms control can be successful, provided the political vision and the institutional structures are present.

---

[16] Urquhart, B., 'Conflict resolution in 1988: the role of the United Nations', *SIPRI Yearbook 1989* (note 1), chapter 13, p. 446.

[17] Deger, S., 'Disarmament, security and development: a research agenda', paper presented at the International Conference on Defence and Development in South East Asia, Bangkok, Jan. 1990.

9. The debt crisis: economic security

I. Introduction: the lost decade

As the 1980s drew to a close it became apparent that for many Third World countries, particularly in Africa and Latin America, this was a 'lost decade' in terms of welfare and growth. The post-war period has generally been characterized by sustainable growth of per capita income, disturbed by occasional cyclical fluctuations; even during the oil price rise of the 1970s, Third World countries managed to protect their international economic position, principally through the

Table 9.1. The Third World external debt, selected regions, 1982–90

Figures are in US $b. (current prices).

Region	1982	1984	1986	1988	1990
Africa	121.4	133.0	171.3	199.8	206.0
Latin America and the Caribbean	331.2	358.2	383.6	402.7	417.5
Total debt	**826.6**	**918.3**	**1 086.7**	**1 197.2**	**1 246.3**
Total debt-service payments	**135.8**	**136.1**	**144.8**	**170.0**	**175.8**

Source: International Monetary Fund, *World Economic Outlook*, Oct. 1989.

recycling of petro-dollars. For the first time in around 40 years, however, long-term per capita growth rates have turned negative for many developing countries, implying a rapid decline in the standard of living of the majority of their populations. As a tragic irony, this occurred at a time when most industrialized countries experienced some expansion and some developing economies achieved a relatively high stage of development. A major contributory factor towards this decline has been the debt crisis that has bedevilled the Third World for almost the entire decade of the 1980s (see table 9.1). The security implications of this international debt problem have become increasingly crucial.

In terms of international strategic relations, the end of the decade shows a remarkable and positive transformation. Peaceful solutions

Table 9.2. Third World per capita growth of GDP, selected regions, 1981–88

Figures are percentages.[a]

Region	1981–86	1987	1988	Change 1981–88
Sub-Saharan Africa	– 2.6	– 4.5	– 0.4	– 16.3
Latin America and the Caribbean	– 0.7	– 0.6	– 0.6	– 4.7
East Asia	+ 6.7	+ 7.0	+ 7.9	+ 59.4
Highly indebted countries	– 1.2	– 0.6	– 0.6	– 7.1

[a] (–) decline in per capita income; (+) increase in per capita income.

Source: *The World Bank Annual Report 1989* (World Bank: Washington, DC, 1989); authors' calculations.

are being found to old conflicts, particularly in Europe, and the two superpowers have embarked on the path of *détente*. It is tempting to believe that global security will continue to improve and that conflicting issues increasingly will be resolved by peaceful negotiations. Yet if the socio-economic status of the world's poor continues to deteriorate in the next decade, the prospects for true peace are not good. The non-military dimensions of security will become increasingly important. If food, development and environment needs continue not to be met, a different form of conflict will emerge. If the trends established in this decade are allowed to continue, there is reason to be more cautious when speaking about the future of peace.

The President of the World Bank, Barber Conable, said in 1988: 'The stubborn fact of the Eighties is that growth has been inadequate, poverty is still on the rise and the environment poorly protected. Unchanged, these realities would deny our children a peaceful, decent and livable world'.[1] The facts bear out this gloomy prognosis. Throughout the 1980s the regions of sub-Saharan Africa as well as Latin America and the Caribbean experienced a negative growth rate in their per capita GDP. The level of *real* (after adjusting for inflation) income per head in 1988 for sub-Saharan Africa was 17 per cent less than in 1981. The corresponding figure for Latin America (and the Caribbean) was around 5 per cent; and for the highly indebted countries, over 7 per cent. By contrast, in East Asia the income per

---

[1] Quoted in United Nations Children's Fund, *The State Of the World's Children 1989* (Oxford University Press: Oxford, 1989).

Table 9.3. Third World long-term debt, financial flows, official development assistance and arms imports, 1984–88[a]

Figures are in US $b.

Year	Total debt	Debt-service	Principal	Interest	Net transfer	ODA[b]	Arms imports
1984	686.7	101.8	48.6	53.2	– 10.2	28.7	41.9
1986	893.9	116.4	61.5	54.9	– 28.7	36.7	32.6
1988	993.2	142.4	75.4	67.0	– 50.1	48.1	30.8

[a] Debt-service is expressed in total and as principal and interest. Net transfer is the remainder of new loans minus debt-service.

[b] Official development assistance from Western countries.

Sources: *The World Bank Annual Report 1989* (World Bank: Washington, DC, 1989); US Arms Control and Disarmament Agency, *World Military Expenditures and Arms Transfers 1988* (US Government Printing Office: Washington, DC, 1989); Organization for Economic Co-operation and Development, *Development Co-operation in the 1990s* (OECD: Paris, 1989); authors' estimates.

head rose by around 60 per cent during the same period.[2] The last column of table 9.2 shows the approximate decline of per capita income of various regional groupings of countries.

There are many reasons why the global economic crisis has had such a heavy impact on Third World economies. The most catastrophic element has been the debt crisis, which has affected many developing countries throughout the decade. Table 9.3 presents statistics for long-term debt. Of particular interest here is the negative transfer of resources. Owing to accumulated debt, the Third World countries as a whole are now paying back to the First World in excess of $50 billion more than they receive in new money. To put it bluntly, the poor are subsidizing the rich.

By the late 1970s the international financial system had at its disposal large amounts of surplus funds from the oil-producing countries which it lent at low rates of interest. In 1981 the incoming Reagan Administration decided on the largest peacetime military expenditure programme in the history of the USA. This huge increase in government expenditure was financed by borrowing on the international money market rather than through taxation or money creation. This led to a rapid rise in interest rates and an over-valuation of the dollar.

[2] For details see *The World Bank Annual Report 1989* (World Bank: Washington, DC, 1989).

World interest rates rose in response, and the burden of debt-servicing for the Third World increased dramatically.

Since 1982, when Mexico failed to meet its debt-servicing obligation,[3] the debt crisis has passed through three phases. The first phase focused on the possibility that a major debtor country would default or refuse to pay interest or capital. The second phase was associated with the fear that individual banks were vulnerable to non-payment of debt obligations. Both of these risks were averted by schemes which protected the international money system. The third phase has now begun and will be characterized by very heavy damage to the economy of the debtors. These countries face major social, political and economic difficulties as they struggle to service their debts.[4] The central problem is how to earn enough foreign exchange to pay the interests that have accrued. The cost of interest payment in the 1980s was *over five times* that of the 1970s.[5] In their scramble to increase exports, debtors have diverted their national output from domestic consumption and investment. Consumer goods and food have been sold abroad, poverty alleviation programmes have been stopped, investment has declined, capital stock is ageing, and growth has fallen.[6]

In spite of the economic concepts which are used to describe and solve the debt problem, the essential elements of a solution must lie in political factors. Unless or until the political will is present, whereby

[3] The origins of the debt crisis are discussed in Nunnenkamp, P., *The International Debt Crisis of the Third World: Causes and Consequences* (Wheatsheaf Books: Brighton, E. Sussex, 1986).

[4] As table 9.3 shows, interest payment is around 50 per cent of total debt-servicing.

[5] See Deger, S., 'World military expenditure', SIPRI, *SIPRI Yearbook 1989: World Armaments and Disarmament* (Oxford University Press: Oxford, 1989), p. 177, note 103. See also Congdon, T., *The Debt Threat* (Basil Blackwell: Oxford, 1988).

[6] The Latin American debt problem and its implications for the domestic economies are discussed in Griffith-Jones, S. and Sunkel, O., *Debt and Development Crises in Latin America: The End of an Illusion* (Clarendon Press: Oxford, 1986). Recent economic problems of nine Latin American countries are discussed in *Economic Panorama of Latin America 1988* (Economic Commission for Latin America and the Caribbean: Santiago de Chile, 1988). The security implications of debt in Latin America are explored in the US Congressional Report *Economic Development in Latin America and the Debt Problem*, Selected Essays prepared for the Joint Economic Committee, US Congress (US Government Printing Office: Washington, DC, 1987); see in particular Mayio, A., 'Economic and political development in South America: the new style military regimes 1964–1985', pp. 275–327; and Vaky, V.P., 'Political change in Latin America: a foreign policy dilemma for the United States', pp. 328–36. There are numerous analyses of the socio-economic crisis in Africa, particularly for sub-Saharan Africa. One of the most perceptive is the report published in 1989 by the UN Economic Commission for Africa, *African Alternative Framework to Structural Adjustment Programmes* (ECA: Addis Ababa, 1989). For a detailed description of the African social and economic problems emanating from external debt, focusing on the role of the World Bank

the main economic powers accept the need for a permanent solution without destroying the debtors, there will be little chance of resolution of this issue. As Professor Rudiger Dornbusch puts it, 'solving debt problems is mostly politics, not economics'.[7] The first formal recognition of this was offered in 1989 by the US Government. The Brady Plan (named after US Treasury Secretary Nicholas Brady) marks the first acceptance of debt forgiveness as an important option for selected Third World countries.[8] The USA has thereby acknowledged that situations exist in which borrowing countries may be unable to complete repayments of massive debts. In addition, the Brady Plan also points to the crucial importance of political and strategic factors. The three countries for which a solution is being sought, with the powerful backing of the US Government, are Costa Rica, Mexico and the Philippines. Media analysis has clearly focused on the security implications of helping these countries: 'All US efforts have been directed at securing an early agreement—not only because Mexico is the second largest debtor but also because of its geographic position on America's southern border. National security considerations have never been far from the surface'; in similar fashion, 'Costa Rica would not normally be a priority for international banks. That it is third in line for the Brady treatment shows in large part the country's importance in terms of foreign policy, as a close political ally to the United States in Central America'.[9] All three countries are of major strategic importance for US defence and foreign policy; hence they need to be helped.

and the IMF, see Onimode, B. (ed.), *The IMF, The World Bank and African Debt*, vol. 1: *The Economic Impact* and vol. 2: *The Social and Political Impact* (Zed Books: London, 1989).

[7] Dornbusch, R., *Dollars, Debts and Deficits* (MIT Press: Cambridge, Mass., 1986).

[8] For details and analysis of the Brady Plan, see *Financial Times*, 11–12 Mar. 1989; 'Approaches to debt reduction', *Finance and Development*, vol. 26, no. 3 (Sep. 1989), p. 16; 'Acid test for Brady Plan', *Stuttgarter Zeitung*, 25 July 1989; 'IMF/World Bank meetings: bye, bye, Brady', *The Economist*, 30 Sep. 1989 p. 96; Zawadzky, K, 'Changing course in the debt srategy', *Development and Cooperation*, no. 3 (1989), p. 27.

[9] Details on IMF participation in the Brady Plan for the three countries (as well as initial support for Venezuela) are given in Dooley, M. and Watson, C. M., 'Reinvigorating the debt strategy', *Finance and Development*, Sep. 1989, pp. 8–11. The agreement on Mexico is analysed in *Financial Times*, 25 July 1989, p. 3, from which the quotation is taken. The agreement with Costa Rica within the same framework is discussed in *Financial Times*, 30 Oct. 1989, p. 3.

II. Official development assistance and military expenditure of donor countries

There are three distinct causes of the current debt crisis. First, there are domestic issues in Third World countries themselves; these are discussed in section III. Second, the global economic climate in this decade has produced a number of adverse factors which have seriously affected developing countries. The structurally weak economies have been incapable of handling these external shocks, some of which have been severe. Faced with the adverse political and electoral consequences of high inflation at the beginning of the decade, most Western governments—particularly in Europe—cut down aggregate demand and controlled monetary growth. The fall in demand led to a collapse in commodity prices, the main export earner for many poor countries. At the same time, the price of Third World imports from the industrial countries remained stable. Thus the terms of trade—the price of Third World exports relative to the price of imports—have fallen rapidly, leading to high borrowing in order to finance minimum requirements for imported goods, in particular for indispensable machinery.

However, the single most important factor in exacerbating world debt has been governmental budgetary policy in the USA. The financing of defence spending under the Reagan Administration, through excessive reliance on borrowing, has made the USA the largest debtor country in the world.[10] President Bush's first budget, presented in February 1989, estimated the FY 1989 federal budget deficit to be about $160 billion.[11] The aggregate outstanding debt of the Government in 1989 exceeded $2000 billion, of which about $300 billion were owed to foreign lenders. In 1989 probably the first significant turn-around occurred in US Government thinking on the budgetary imbalance. Although increases in taxation still remain taboo (and the President has fought a bruising battle with Congress about reducing capital gains tax), ambitious plans have been put forward to reduce significantly military expenditure in the medium term (FY 1992–95).[12]

---

[10] The foreign debt of the USA, the world's largest debtor country, was $533 billion at the end of 1988; see *International Herald Tribune*, 30 June 1988, p. 11.

[11] *Congressional Quarterly*, 11 Feb. 1989, p. 248.

[12] US Defense Secretary Richard Cheney's plans to reduce US military expenditure through force cuts and procurement reductions are discussed in chapter 5.

Table 9.4. Current account balance of selected trading countries, 1986–90
Figures are in US $b.

	1986	1987	1988	1989	1990
Japan	85.8	87.0	79.6	72.0	89.7
FR Germany	39.4	45.2	48.6	53.4	56.8
Asian NICs	23.2	30.3	27.8	26.1	25.0
Total of surplus countries	**148.4**	**165.2**	**156.0**	**151.5**	**171.5**
USA	– 133.3	– 143.7	– 126.5	– 125.1	– 138.7
UK	– 0.2	– 4.8	– 26.0	– 30.6	– 26.7
Total of deficit countries	**– 133.1**	**– 148.4**	**– 152.5**	**– 155.7**	**– 165.4**

Source: International Monetary Fund, *World Economic Outlook*, Oct. 1989.

However, neither the level of US defence spending nor the US budget deficit in itself constitutes the main problem in this regard. The indirect effect of these factors has been more pernicious in that they have created a huge trade deficit, with imports far exceeding exports. This external imbalance can only be financed by international capital flows to the USA, which in turn has deprived other countries of foreign exchange. In 1981 the USA had a current account (export minus import) surplus of about $6.9 billion; in 1987 the *deficit* was of the order of $144 billion.[13] Although the deficit fell somewhat by 1989, the level is forecasted to peak again in 1990.

Traditionally, developed countries have had foreign trade surpluses (exports greater than imports) which have been utilized to finance the deficits (imports greater than exports) of developing nations. At earlier stages of development, countries have imported machineries and other investment goods to foster growth; this leads to external deficits which are financed by foreign borrowing. This trend was reversed in the 1980s with the USA (and to a lesser extent the UK) soaking up the financial capital surplus produced globally. The major trade surplus countries in 1989 are Japan, the Federal Republic of Germany and the four Asian so-called newly industrializing countries (NICs): Hong Kong, Singapore, South Korea and Taiwan. Table 9.4 shows how the trade surplus of these countries is almost exactly absorbed by the USA and the UK combined, leaving little for the rest of the world. In a

[13] International Monetary Fund, *World Economic Outlook* (IMF: Washington, DC, Oct. 1989).

Table 9.5. Official development assistance as share of GNP and military expenditure, and military expenditure as share of GDP: major donor countries, 1988

Figures are percentages.

Country	ODA/GNP[a]	ODA/Milex[b]	Milex/GDP[c]
Canada	0.49	23.7	2.0
France	0.72	19.0	3.8
FR Germany	0.39	13.6	2.9
Italy	0.39	15.6	2.5
Japan	0.32	32.0	1.0
UK	0.32	7.6	4.3
USA	0.21	3.4	6.1
USSR	0.30	2.6	11.5

[a] Official development assistance as proportion of GNP; OECD figures.
[b] Official development assistance as proportion of military expenditure.
[c] Military expenditure as proportion of GDP.

Source: Organization for Economic Co-operation and Development, *Development Co-operation in the 1990s* (OECD: Paris, 1989); SIPRI data base; authors' calculations.

sense the Third World is being starved of funds owing to the excessive imports (consumption) of these two major powers.

Many of these issues were forcefully reiterated in the Report of the Independent Commission on Financial Flows (known as the Schmidt Commission after its Chairman, former FRG Chancellor Helmut Schmidt) presented in 1989.[14] One innovative element was the strong emphasis on official development assistance (ODA), potentially a major vehicle of help to the Third World that developed countries in both West and East could provide. In particular, ODA can be increased through the 'disarmament dividend', as a conduit to the Third World for some of the resources released through the reductions in military expenditure that are the result of arms control negotiations.

SIPRI has estimated the increase in the value of ODA that could be provided if modest reductions in military expenditure by the major powers were transferred as aid. A 10 per cent reduction in the annual military expenditure of the EC, the USA and Japan together would permit a doubling of the total volume of assistance currently provided by the West. By reducing its defence spending by as little as 1 per

[14] *Facing One World*, Report by an Independent Group on Financial Flows to Developing Countries (Chairman Helmut Schmidt), 1 June 1989.

cent, the USA would release sufficient funds to increase its ODA by 29 per cent. A similar 1 per cent reduction and transfer would allow the USSR to raise its development assistance by 39 per cent.

Total ODA from the Western nations and Japan is around $48 billion per year. The share of ODA as a proportion of GNP is still quite low for major donor countries and is generally far below the 0.7 per cent set as a target by the United Nations.[15] The figures for France fall substantially—to around 0.5 per cent—if its overseas territory recipients are excluded. For the USA the share is extremely low, even though it is the largest donor by actual size. Japan is set to become the largest donor country by 1990. The data on the ratio of ODA to military expenditure are also revealing (table 9.5). They demonstrate the extent to which major powers, such as the USA, the USSR and the UK, provide very little foreign aid relative to their massive defence spending. Once again, a slight re-allocation of resources would make a substantial contribution to global economic security.

III. Security, development and democracy

In terms of debt-servicing (payment of principal and interest), the Third World now pays back more to the industrialized nations than it receives. As mentioned above, there is now a net transfer of resources from poor to rich countries. Between 1983 and 1987 Latin America paid back about $90 billion more to developed countries than it received. Such negative transfers are unprecedented in the whole history of financial transactions.

The worst domestic effect of Third World debt comes from the fact that much of it is concentrated in government hands. Unless there is a government bankruptcy, which is not conceivable, the payments on obligations will be made. Thus government expenditure has to be reduced in other fields if debt-servicing is to be maintained. Spending on health, education, infrastructure, economic development, food subsidies, job creation and poverty alleviation is therefore reduced. Since the state is the major provider in these areas in developing countries, the socio-economic effects of such cuts would be devastat-

[15] In 1988, the latest year for which figures are available, total ODA from Western nations (Australia, Canada, Japan, New Zealand, the USA and Western Europe) was $48.1 billion, amounting to 0.35 per cent of the combined GNP of these countries. See also Wheeler, J., 'The critical role for official development assistance in the 1990s', *Finance and Development*, Sep. 1989, pp. 39–40.

ing. Former President Julius Nyerere of Tanzania puts it starkly: 'Must we starve our children to pay our debts?'[16]

It is often thought that some of the problems of the Third World are self-inflicted. In particular, it is held that high military expenditures constitute a drain on resources, and that savings can be made here to pay for welfare services. This is partly true—some of the high debt burdens are associated with arms imports and government deficits to finance defence spending. In many of the highly indebted countries, such as Argentina, Brazil and the Philippines, new democratic governments are paying the price of the high defence spending of previous military governments.[17]

A major reason for international indebtedness has also been the import of arms, much of which was financed by borrowing during the 1970s. According to the SIPRI arms trade data base, the volume of major weapons transferred to the Third World (excluding China) more than doubled between 1970 and 1980.[18] Using US price indices, the dollar value of arms transferred at current prices would mean a four-fold increase in weapon imports during this period. With both the USA and the USSR striving to earn foreign exchange during this period, a substantial part of this import by the Third World could have been debt-financed.[19] It is difficult to make estimates of the burden of debt arising out of weapon purchases, but it is thought to be significant. Earlier estimates show that around 20 per cent of Third World debt until around 1980 was due to arms imports alone.[20] In 1989 World Bank President Barber Conable estimated that a full one-third of the debt of some major Third World countries can be attributed to arms imports.[21] The profligacy of military governments, which were

[16] Note 1, p. 30.

[17] For a critical evaluation of military spending in Argentina during the military dictatorships of the 1970s, see the World Bank country study *Argentina: Economic Memorandum* (World Bank: Washington, DC, 1985).

[18] See *SIPRI Yearbook 1989* (note 5), appendix 6A, pp. 226–29.

[19] For an evaluation of Soviet hard currency earnings from arms sales, see Kanet, R. E., 'Soviet and East European arms transfers to the Third World: strategic, political and economic factors', *External Relations of CMEA Countries: Their Significance and Impact in a Global Perspective, NATO Colloquium 1983* (NATO: Brussels, 1983), pp. 171–94. A more theoretical analysis is conducted in Deger, S., 'The economics of Soviet arms trade', ed. R. Cassen, *Soviet Relations in the Third World* (Royal Institute of International Affairs, Sage: London, 1989), pp. 159–76.

[20] The figure is derived in Brzoska, M., 'The military-related debt of Third World countries', *Journal of Peace Research*, vol. 20, no. 3 (1983), pp. 271–77.

[21] *Defense and Economy World Report*, issue 1152 (13 Dec. 1989), p. 6535.

the rule rather than the exception during the 1970s, has come to haunt today's democratic leaders.

In recent years many Third World countries have made significant progress towards democratization, with constitutional governments elected in free, multi-party elections. In Asia, Pakistan and the Philippines now enjoy civilian governments after years of military rule. In Africa, Nigeria is expected to have a non-military government in 1992. The most dramatic shift towards democratic ideals, however, is in Latin America, where free elections are being held and where non-military governments are now the rule rather than the exception. In Argentina, Brazil and Chile, three of the region's major powers, constitutional governments were elected in 1989. However, if democracy also implies political participation to achieve social and economic equity, then these new regimes have none the less failed. As the food riots of Venezuela and the attempted military *coup* in the Philippines showed in 1989, the foundations for a stable democracy are still weak. In his inaugural speech in December 1988, President Carlos Salinas de Gortari warned: 'In economic stagnation, democracy would fade'. The debt crisis has been a major cause of instability for these young democracies, which might yet fail to achieve political maturity.[22]

A positive development is that military expenditure has been falling in the Third World since around 1985. As a result of both the resolution of conflicts and economic constraints, governments have sought to reduce the burden of defence. As 1990 approached, inter-state conflicts were on the decline—as witnessed by the cease-fire in the Iraq–Iran War, the Soviet withdrawal from Afghanistan, relative stability in Southern Africa, and *rapprochement* in the Horn of Africa and the Maghreb.

On the other hand, there is now a corresponding growth of subnationalism, with the legitimacy of central government and even of the nation-state as such, increasingly called into question: the Palestinian *intifada* on the West Bank and Gaza Strip, anti-apartheid movements conducted by the church in South Africa, narcotic traffickers in Colombia, guerrilla movements in Peru, army revolts in

---

[22] For a perceptive analysis of the relationship between debt and democracy, see Graham, C. L., 'The Latin American quagmire: beyond debt and democracy', *Brookings Review*, vol. 7, no. 2 (spring 1989), pp. 42–47. The political economy of debt is also emphasized in 'Need to staunch the haemorrage', *Financial Times*, 2 Feb. 1989, from which the quotation is taken.

Table 9.6. Official development assistance as share of GNP and military expenditure, and military expenditure as share of GDP: selected recipient countries, 1986–87

Figures are percentages.

Country	ODA/GNP[a]	ODA/Milex[b]	Milex/GDP[c]
Argentina	0.3	3.6	3.4
Chile	0.05	1.7	6.8
China	0.5	12.8	4.0
Costa Rica	5.7	632.9	0.7
Egypt	4.7	35.1	6.2
El Salvador	10.2	241.0	3.8
India	1.1	19.2	3.8
Israel	6.2	25.6	9.0
Ivory Coast	2.9	125.0	1.2
Mozambique	16.7	159.0	10.5
Nicaragua	2.3	5.2	44.1
Nigeria	0.3	32.9	1.0
Pakistan	2.6	33.7	6.8
Paraguay	1.5	167.2	1.1
Peru	1.2	13.2	8.0
Zaire	10.7	1 389	1.3
Zimbabwe	5.1	74.1	6.5

[a] 1986–87 average official development assistance as proportion of 1986 GNP; OECD figures.

[b] 1987 official development assistance as a proportion of military expenditure.

[c] 1987 military expenditure as proportion of GDP; not strictly comparable with the first column.

Source: Organization for Economic Co-operation and Development, *Development Co-operation* (OECD: Paris, 1988); SIPRI data base; authors' calculations.

Argentina, lawlessness among Afghan migrants in Pakistan and ethnic violence in Sri Lanka are just a few examples of intra-state conflicts that were of major concern in 1989.[23] Many of these instances are traceable to developmental failures and the inability of the 'haves' to buy off the 'have-nots'.

---

[23] See also Lindgren, K., Wilson, G. K., Wallensteen, P. and Nordquist, K-Å., 'Major armed conflicts in 1989', in SIPRI, *SIPRI Yearbook 1990: World Armaments and Disarmament* (Oxford University Press: Oxford, 1990), chapter 10. The growing concern in the USA about the events in Colombia, and the threat to the legitimacy of the state from narcotics dealers, led to military aid being appropriated to an internal security issue. It has been suggested that funds saved from cutting US military expenditure should be diverted towards such forms of security assistance to combat drug-related terrorism.

Just as military expenditure is a severe drain on resources in poor countries, imaginatively utilized ODA can be of crucial help to the Third World. The ratio of ODA to military expenditure among Third World countries contains wide variations, reflecting both specific security concerns and the political relationship between donors and recipients (see table 9.6). For some countries, such as Costa Rica, where military spending is very low, maximum use can be made of ODA. For countries in unstable regional areas, such as Egypt, defence spending is a major drain on resources which ODA cannot hope to replace. The same is true for large countries such as China and India, which receive low levels of assistance compared to their size, yet maintain large military forces to protect regional security interests.

IV. Debt and arms control in the Third World

It is remarkable that in spite of the progress of arms control negotiations in the East–West framework and the usefulness of such a model for stability and security elsewhere, there is no functioning formal arms control mechanism in any Third World conflict situation. The Non-Proliferation Treaty, in the nuclear sphere, is the only modestly successful implementation of arms control that has a Third World dimension. Other attempts, such as in the spheres of chemical and biological weapons, ballistic missiles and conventional weapons trade, have generally ended in failure. The much heralded Conventional Arms Transfer Talks (CATT) in 1977–78 between the USA and the USSR ended in failure both for systemic reasons (pressure from the arms industry at a time of low domestic procurement budgets in the USA) and because of the cooling of international relations between the superpowers.[24] In 1988 and 1989 there was increasing concern over ballistic missile acquisition by major countries in the Third World.[25] However, attempted arms transfer controls have so far failed to deter countries which are determined to acquire such arsenals. Few formal attempts have been made to negotiate, codify and establish CSBMs among Third World countries, either bilaterally or in the context of geographical regional security.

[24] See Husbands, J. L. and Cahn, A. H., 'The Conventional Arms Transfer Talks: an experiment in mutual arms trade restraint', ed. T. Ohlson, SIPRI, *Arms Transfers Limitations and Third World Security* (Oxford University Press: Oxford, 1988), pp. 110–25.
[25] See Karp, A., 'Ballistic missile proliferation', in *SIPRI Yearbook 1990* (note 23).

There are many reasons why such formal arms control mechanisms have failed.[26] As the 1980s drew to a close, however, it became increasingly clear that arms control and disarmament can only be hastened in the Third World through systemic and structural change. Domestic economic problems will force countries to cut back on their military expenditure and procurement budgets, which would have an immediate impact on arms transfers. The major powers could then act as catalysts to speed up the process by non-interference, promotion of co-operative action, emphasis on common security and encouragement of transfer of resources from the military to the civilian sectors.

The process is not fundamentally different from that taking place in the USSR. The Soviet Union has found it increasingly difficult to allocate 10–20 per cent (depending on how the aggregate figures are measured) of its national output to defence. Its attempts at unilateral disarmament and at speeding the arms control negotiation process are indicative of a strong desire to relate domestic re-allocation of scarce resources to a co-operative and peaceful framework for inter-state relations. In the case of the Third World, the socio-economic problems are even more acute and the external threats generally less intimidating. Hence, the desire for arms control may be more intense as the economic crisis tends to take priority over the military security crisis.

The debt burden can therefore be used as a window of opportunity through which in particular Third World countries can reduce military expenditure, concomitant arms procurement and transfer as well as foster an atmosphere of arms control. The combination of high military spending and debt repayment creates an untenable and explosive situation for Third World governments, as they fail to meet the most basic welfare needs of their citizens. For many Third World governments, military expenditure and public external debt-service take an overwhelming proportion of earned revenue (income). As table 9.7 shows, foreign debt repayments and defence for many countries account for 40–80 per cent of current government revenue. This does not take into account private sector debts (sometimes guaranteed by the government), nor does it account for domestic debts, which for some countries are also very high. The amount of resources remaining for all other forms of government expenditure—health, education, social security, economic services, infrastructure, food subsidies and salaries—is very limited after these two major spending categories are

[26] These issues are discussed in Ohlson (note 24).

Table 9.7. Military expenditure and external public debt-service as shares of current government revenue, selected Third World countries, 1987

Figures are percentages.

Country	Military expenditure	External debt-service	Military expenditure plus debt-service
Argentina	15.8	23.6	39.4
Colombia	14.5	50.7	65.2
Chile	22.0	25.6	47.6
Egypt	19.6	11.8	31.4
Indonesia	13.9	35.5	49.4
Israel	30.9	13.1	44.0
Jordan	48.9	36.2	85.1
Morocco	19.5	30.9	50.4
Pakistan	40.1	20.4	60.5
Philippines	15.5	48.1	63.6
Sri Lanka	30.7	24.2	54.9
Zimbabwe	22.5	23.5	46.0

Sources: *World Development Report* (World Bank: Washington, DC, 1989); SIPRI data base; authors' calculations.

financed. The result is a domestic crisis which erodes legitimacy and condemns the masses to greater poverty.

The debt crisis may force Third World governments to re-evaluate their priorities and seriously consider whether their military expenditures have crossed the limits of reasonable sufficiency. SIPRI data indicate that real or inflation-adjusted total military expenditure has declined steadily from around 1985. If the Iraq–Iran War is excluded from the aggregate, the decline is quite sharp. The SIPRI arms trade register for 1989[27] also indicates that the trend indicator value of arms imports by the Third World (excluding China) has also fallen slightly since the peak of the early 1980s.[28] The debt crisis and inadequate financial flows must account at least in part for these signals of arms control. The major military and economic powers can hasten this process by suitable policies which link foreign assistance with progress in arms control in the Third World. At the same time they must be willing to provide more ODA as military spending is reduced following reductions in East–West tensions. The Schmidt Commis-

[27] See *SIPRI Yearbook 1990* (note 23), appendix 7B.
[28] See Deger, S., 'Recent patterns of arms trade and regional conflict', paper presented at the 39th Annual Pugwash Conference, Cambridge, Mass., 23–28 July 1989.

sion made an interesting suggestion that ODA should be increased to countries which have a ceiling of 2 per cent on the share of defence in GDP.[29] Such measures, together with other initiatives such as setting up a disarmament–development fund as suggested in the United Nations, could help promote the demilitarization of the Third World. However, all will be to no avail if development failures, prompted by the debt crisis, increase conflict.

One major problem from a security point of view is that even though total government spending—including defence expenditure—is falling, the share of the military in the total could be rising. Hence, defence expenditure exhibits 'resilience' in the sense that it seems to be protected to some degree—at the expense of other expenditures, such as on welfare—from the ravages of austerity cuts. It should be noted that in countries where the share of defence spending has fallen, the share of internal security spending may be rising, but limited data make it difficult to establish a trend at this stage.

V. Eastern Europe

Eastern Europe experienced remarkable change in 1989 as movements for democratization and political pluralism spread across the region. However, economic problems were also all-pervasive as countries struggled to adjust to the difficulties of restructuring their economies. The debt burden contributed heavily to their problems. The East European debt problem is qualitatively different from that of the Third World. However, many of the issues discussed above have relevance to at least some countries of the region. In particular for Poland and Hungary there exists a close link between security and debt which merits special attention.

The USSR has a large hard currency debt of the order of $41.7 billion in gross terms.[30] Its net debt position is manageable, however, largely due to its export potential to the West of raw materials, in particular oil and natural gas. It also has large reserves of dollar deposits in Western banks; the net value of debt after taking account of such deposits is quite small in relation to the Soviet GNP (about $27.3 billion). In Romania the Ceausescu regime paid off the foreign debt at

---

[29] See note 14.
[30] Johnson, R., 'Western lending to the Soviet Union', paper presented at the Workshop on US–USSR Commercial Relations, sponsored by the Congressional Research Service for the Senate Foreign Relations Committee, US Senate, Washington, DC, 17 Apr. 1989.

the cost of extreme domestic recession and hardship, and for this it later paid the price. As one of its first measures, the new regime reduced exports to satisfy domestic consumption.

Poland and Hungary both have sizeable foreign debts: the ratio of debt to GNP amounts to around 57 and 62 per cent, respectively, for 1988. Particularly in the case of Poland, the burden of debt-servicing is increasing dramatically and has become a major impediment to domestic economic reforms. The aggregate stock of debt now approaches almost 60 per cent of national output; 12 per cent of exports are utilized to service foreign debt alone, leaving a diminished amount to finance essential imports of food and machinery required for welfare and growth.[31]

Poland has requested $1.2 billion from the multilateral institutions, the IMF and the World Bank. In addition, it would like to receive around $1 billion from the Group of Seven countries[32] to maintain its foreign reserves at an adequate level. The latter amount is particularly crucial since there must be confidence in the financial system to prevent a devaluation of the zloty, which would destroy its convertibility and create a financial crisis. IMF conditionality will require a large reduction in the Government's budget deficit. This will predominantly have to come from eliminating subsidies, particularly on food and coal. A substantial rise in food and fuel costs will exacerbate tensions within the country. The possibility of food riots cannot be ruled out. Earlier attempts at reducing subsidies, leading to high prices, led to urban discontent and rioting. The impact on internal security and the fragile democratic process could be substantial.[33]

The amount of foreign assistance and government-backed credit authorized so far by Western countries is quite small. The total amount pledged by the end of 1989 to Eastern Europe (excluding the USSR) is of the order of $4.3 billion. In addition, with the establishment of the European Development Bank at the 1989 EC summit in Strasbourg, it was in principle agreed that the bank immediately be authorized to lend 10 billion European Currency Units (ECUs) (approximately $8.7 billion). Assuming that about $5 billion will be available in the short term from this new financial institution, the total

[31] *Managing the Transition: Integrating the Reforming Socialist Countries into the World Economy*, first year report (Institute for East–West Security Studies: New York, 1989).
[32] Canada, France, the FRG, Italy, Japan, the UK and the USA.
[33] Sachs, J. D., 'Democratic Poland can make it if the West weighs in quickly', *International Herald Tribune*, 31 Oct. 1989.

amount of public foreign capital will still be less than $10 billion. Although it seems a large sum, it is small compared to the debt burden that Eastern Europe currently shoulders. The GDR, Hungary and Poland have an accumulated foreign debt of approximately $78 billion. Although no precise figures are available, preliminary estimates indicate that the debt-service of these three countries could amount to $10 billion per annum. In other words, the total new finance pledged by the West could be eaten up simply by one year's debt repayments.

It is instructive to compare this situation with the period immediately following World War II, when massive amounts of foreign capital were used to rejuvenate the economies of Western Europe and to foster stability and peace. Under the Marshall Plan, the USA provided $12.8 billion to Europe in 1948–52.[34] Most of this money was in the form of grants; the credit element was minimal. The recipients had no earlier burden of debt which needed a reverse transfer of funds. There was little need to restructure markets and try to make them more efficient. None of these favourable conditions is present today in Eastern Europe, yet the financial flows received are insignificant compared to the previous era. In 1989 prices the value of Marshall aid would be $67.5 billion.[35] In contrast, the total amount promised to Eastern Europe at the end of 1989 by Western governments was estimated to have been around $10 billion. Much of it is long-term loans, and its real value is substantially reduced by the demands of debt-servicing. It is also worth noting that in November 1989 President Bush signed the appropriations measures which provide aid authorizations by Congress for financial assistance to Hungary and Poland; in FY 1990 a total of only $532.8 million will be distributed.[36]

There is a close connection between debt and military expenditure in Poland as well. As the total stock of debt has risen, as well as its share in output, military expenditure has declined from the mid-1980s. This is in spite of the perceived threat from NATO's 3 per cent growth rate of defence spending affirmed over the decade. With recent political changes, and the first non-communist government in Eastern Europe, the process of demilitarization is set to continue. Yet, as discussed above, true security and stability will not be possible

[34] See Huhne, C., 'East European changes are chance for historic bargains', *The Guardian*, 13 Dec. 1989.
[35] Estimate, based on the increase in the US GNP deflator between 1950 and 1989.
[36] *Congressional Quarterly*, 18. Nov. 1989, p. 3172.

without economic restructuring. This will require foreign assistance, on relatively easy terms, so that austerity does not destroy the fabric of the society. Ralf Dahrendorf has expressed the general sentiment as follows:

The new democracies need and deserve help in their painful transitions. . . Marshall plan or not, a massive economic recovery programme for Eastern Europe is the only way to prove that we do not respond to Eastern abuses of power with Western selfishness of prosperity (to quote from a plea by Countess Dönhoff and ex-Chancellor Schmidt in the West German weekly *Die Zeit*).[37]

VI. Conclusion

Speaking before a joint session of Congress on 15 November 1989, Lech Walesa, leader of the Polish Solidarity independent trade union, said that aid 'is the best investment in the future and in peace, better than tanks, warships and warplanes, an investment leading to greater security'.[38]

Unless the recent trends of economic crisis are reversed, conflicts will continue. Their underlying causes, however, will increasingly be developmental failures rather than political actions. The catalyst will be the difference between actual growth and expected growth, and the inability of debtor governments to meet the aspirations of major sections of their populations. Unless the security implications of the debt crisis are fully understood, and political solutions take precedence over economic technicalities, the recent dawn of peace may be darkened by new clouds of conflict.

[37] Dahrendorf, R., 'A revolution to tumble barricades', *The Observer*, 19 Nov. 1989.
[38] Dahrendorf (note 37).

10. Conclusion: the disarmament dividend

I. A new world?

World military expenditure in 1989 was of the order of $950 billion. However, both military expenditure and militarization are now on the decline. Structural reasons related to technological and economic factors are as important as those related to political change. Disarmament, deficits, dollars, development and debt all interrelate with politics, personalities, passion and policy to produce a complex set of causes and effects. There is great hope that structural and political factors have coalesced at the same moment to continue the impetus towards controlling the military expenditure process.

As political differences converge, large-scale military conflicts become less viable and military doctrines accommodate to new realities, the question arises as to the type of 'defence' that will be the future norm. Thomas Schelling argued that weapon systems embody an inherent propensity towards war or peace.[1] In current terminology these could be termed offensive and defensive weapons, although the distinction is usually blurred and the perception is different from reality. Clearly, with the disappearance of major threats, the former types of weapon will become unnecessary and major cost savings will be possible.

The central problem in the future lies with those armaments which promote 'active' defence—trying to intercept and destroy the enemy's weapons (such as bombers, missiles or submarines) before they are used.[2] However, such essentially defensive measures provoke countermeasures in the form of more sophisticated offensive forces. Thus, anti-ballistic missiles lead to the creation of multiple independently targeted re-entry vehicles; major improvements in radar technology prompt the creation of 'stealth' and second-strike bombers

---

[1] See Schelling, T., *Arms and Influence* (Yale University Press: New Haven, 1966); for a formal analysis, see Anderton, C. H., 'The inherent propensity toward peace or war embodied in weaponry', *Defence Economics*, vol. 1, no. 3 (1990), pp. 197–220.

[2] Lakoff, S. and York, H. F., *A Shield in Space? Technology, Politics and the Strategic Defense Initiative* (University of California Press: Berkeley, 1989).

such as the B-2; airborne early-warning aircraft could be destroyed by the 'stealth' fighter currently being developed; defensive systems capable of intercepting attacks from manually operated weapons are not immune to 'smart' weapons, for example, the short-range attack missiles which can be released by pilots without penetrating enemy defence systems; and as submarines become more silent and almost impossible to detect, their destructive capacity becomes many times stronger than in the past (a D-5 missile installed in the Trident submarine has almost the same capability as the MX missile). The list is ominously long.

As arms control negotiations near fruition, and the first CFE as well as START agreements lead on to further rounds of weapon reductions, the quantitative arms dynamic is set to slow down. There is every reason to believe that arms procurement will be substantially reduced in the future and armed forces will be at much lower levels. As mentioned in chapter 1, the forces of TESD coupled with recent political changes could be sufficient to curtail various components of military expenditure, and the world military system will have substantially lower weapon stocks. The beneficial implications for international security are obvious. What is not so clear is the future course of R&D and the effects of the technological arms race which could enhance the quality of weapon systems at exactly the same time as quantities are being cut.

World expenditure on military R&D is now estimated to be around $94 billion or about 10 per cent of world defence spending. Over 80 per cent is accounted for by the two superpowers (in comparable prices). Planned reductions in defence-related research are of much lower orders of magnitude than in other components of the military budgets of the major powers. In spite of revolutionary changes in the political order, there is significant concern about transferring resources from military to civilian research. Indeed the potential for *reconversion* is strong since governments and defence industrial organizations maintain substantial military research capabilities while at the same time reducing personnel, closing bases and mothballing equipment.

The two central issues for the next decade will be to control the use (or misuse) of technology for military purposes and to tackle non-military threats to global security. The first relates to the industrial world (both East and West); the second relates mainly to developments in the Third World but whose effects spill over to developed countries. There are a number of non-military security problems: population pressures, ethnic clashes, religious fundamentalism, competition for natural resources and environmental degradation. These factors are causing conflicts within states. Such conflicts may replace inter-state wars as a major source of instability. However, the fundamental problem for the Third World, underlying these conflicts, is developmental failure and lack of economic security. The other issues are catalysts which hasten the implicit conflict generated by poor economic performance and poverty. If the world economy cannot generate the conditions for growth and prosperity, then the prospects for peace are limited.

These twin issues—of technology misuse and underdevelopment—will also affect the course of future military expenditure. Defence spending may rise after a fall if the trends persist. Technology will exert a pull, and as budgets are eased after some time the very existence of advanced weapon blueprints will be an incentive to produce them. In similar fashion, conflicts generated by maldevelopment will make security spending rise again. If these problems can actually be solved, and the agenda is as daunting as was keeping global peace over the past 45 years, then truly we can claim to have achieved a 'new world'.

II. Disarmament dividend or peace penalty?

At present discussions are taking place in many forums about the 'disarmament dividend'. As the discussions spread to countries throughout the world, the expectations and interpretations of the disarmament dividend tend to change. For the USA, it principally means balancing the budget deficit and probably meeting some of the social needs generated by the Reagan era. For West Europeans, it implies more resources for social services and industrial restructuring after the anticipated decline in the defence industries. For the USSR, its effect is to get rid of the huge defence machine which has threatened the existence of the civilian economy. The Third World needs more economic aid and funds from international institutions to get out of the debt trap and away from negative resource transfers. For China, it means economic modernization whose spin-off could produce a leaner but fitter defence sector.

In addition, the question of the 'peace penalty' should also be considered. What if the beneficial effects of peace and disarmament are overwhelmed by certain negative features?

1. The costs of implementing arms control measures—verification, elimination of weapons, resettlement of forces, closure of bases, provision of social security benefits to communities at risk, granting subsidies for industrial restructuring, new investments for conversion and coping with higher unemployment—could be high, even though they occur once and for all.

2. There will be greater competition for global resources as East European countries enter international financial markets. Thus resources for the Third World might be 'crowded out' and economic development will suffer, causing conflicts to increase.

3. The major powers may become more inward looking and lose interest in the rest of the world, particularly the developing countries.

4. As arms procurement in the industrial economies declines, there exists an incentive to export. The Third World then could reap a particularly pernicious form of the 'peace penalty'.

No doubt the current peace process and disarmament will be beneficial, even if not in the way it is always expected to be. At least it has brought to the minds of many the ultimate absurdity of amassing weaponry in the name of security while at the same time making the world politically and economically insecure. The long-term effects are structural in nature.[3] High military expenditure, captive markets for arms industries, technological progress which has little direct spin-off, best-quality R&D utilized for weapons, continuation of conflicts, and wasted resources for fighting wars all create distortions in the world economy and make the international political system unstable. Positive changes will therefore have beneficial effects. Co-operative solutions to security problems will also allow leaders the time and effort required to remove structural impediments from the international economic system.

In the more immediate future the most tangible benefits from arms control will have to come from reduced military expenditure and the transfer of resources to other purposes. Since defence spending is all

---

[3] See *Study on the Relationship between Disarmament and Development*, UN Document A/36/356, 5 Oct. 1981; this report was prepared by a group of experts under Ambassador Inga Thorsson and is commonly called the Thorsson Report. See also Deger, S. and West, R., *Defence Security and Development* (Frances Pinter Publishers: London, 1987).

Table 10.1. Costing for environmental defence and social welfare in terms of military spending

Environmental and social needs	Costs in terms of 1988 military spending
A. *Environmental defence* *(annual costs)*	
1. UN Action Plan over 5 years to save world's tropical forests	18 days of Japanese milex
2. Annual cost to clear up hazardous waste sites in the EC by the year 2000	4 days of EC milex
3. UN Action Plan to halt Third World desertification	6 days of US milex
B. *Social welfare in the Third World* *(annual costs)*	
1. Safe water and sanitation (one-half of world's population)	5 days of world milex
2. Supplementary feeding programme (prevent malnutrition)	1 day of world milex
3. Immunization for all children (prevent 1 million deaths per year)	9 hours of world milex

done by governments, they will have to decide on alternatives based on new priorities. In addition, financial resources, being the most fungible can be transferred and rapidly re-allocated, provided the political will is there. Thus far there has been no significant reduction in military expenditure among the major alliances except in restructuring their own defence sectors. If they can restructure military expenditure in a short period of time, then the released resources can be utilized for economic development. This is the fundamental rationale behind the 'disarmament dividend'.

There are many needs that must be satisfied through resource transfers. Even though the first impulse of governments is to look after domestic needs, the international dimensions of the disarmament dividend are vital. If short-sighted policies ignore international economic development, then conflicts will continue, particularly in the Third World, and the peace process will fail. It is therefore imperative to seriously consider how such resource transfers could potentially benefit some of the socio-economic problems of the world's poor. In addition, there is now great concern for environmental protection, which will also require government funding.

Table 10.1 provides some representative data which cost specific environmental and developmental projects and show the equivalent in terms of military spending by various countries and regions. All non-military costs are annual for the project specified; military spending values are expressed in terms of time periods. The purpose is to provide an economic and financial perspective to priorities between military and non-military security and threat. The data make it quite clear that great improvements can be made in the quality of life for the whole world, rich or poor, through modest resource transfers. With greater political vision, much can be achieved.

This book does not suggest that there is an *automatic* link between military expenditure reductions and resource transfers. However, if it is the same agency—the government—which is responsible for both these functions, then in principle such re-allocations are possible. What is really required is *political will*. It is also crucial to actually quantify the amount of the peace dividend and its alternative uses so that informed choices can be made. This is the purpose of table 10.1.

It is still early to conclude whether the disarmament dividend or the peace penalty will dominate in the near future.[4] However, in the long term the former must be the most important as structural changes lead to a more peaceful and stable world and political will is harnessed to solve non-military security problems. Conflicts, in their many forms, remain; possibly among allies on economic issues, but certainly in the Third World where security cannot be defined without taking into account developmental failures. Environmental defence, and protecting the global common, are also of overriding concern. It is to these cases that attention must turn; otherwise global security will not be meaningful and world security expenditure will again resume its upward trend.

[4] For a perceptive statement on North–South relations in the 1990s, in the context of improving East–West relations, see Stützle, W., 'Introduction: More questions than answers—how to manage the change', SIPRI, *World Armaments and Disarmament: SIPRI Yearbook 1990* (Oxford University Press: Oxford, 1990), p. xxxi.

Appendix A. Tables of world military expenditure

SAADET DEGER and SOMNATH SEN, assisted by Carl-Gustaf Lagergren, Phitsamone Ljungqvist-Souvannavong and Fredrik Wetterqvist

Sources and methods are explained in appendix B.

Table A1. World military expenditure, in current price figures, 1980–89

Figures are in local currency, current prices.

		1980	1981	1982	1983	1984	1985	1986	1987	1988	1989
NATO											
North America											
Canada	m. dollars	5 499	6 289	7 655	8 562	9 519	10 187	10 811	11 529	12 180	12 542
USA	m. dollars	143 981	169 888	196 390	218 084	238 136	263 900	282 868	289 391	294 901	302 294
Europe											
Belgium	m. francs	115 754	125 689	132 127	136 615	139 113	144 183	152 079	155 422	150 647	155 164
Denmark	m. kroner	9 117	10 301	11 669	12 574	13 045	13 343	13 333	14 647	15 620	15 813
France	m. francs	111 672	129 708	148 021	165 029	176 638	186 715	197 080	209 525	215 073	223 868
FR Germany	m. D. marks	48 518	52 193	54 234	56 496	57 274	58 649	60 130	61 354	61 638	63 269
Greece	m. drachmas	96 975	142 865	176 270	193 340	271 922	321 981	338 465	393 052	479 236	521 209
Italy	b. lire	8 203	9 868	12 294	14 400	16 433	18 584	20 071	23 788	26 590	28 653
Luxembourg	m. francs	1 534	1 715	1 893	2 104	2 234	2 265	2 390	2 730	3 163	3 142
Netherlands	m. guilders	10 476	11 296	11 921	12 149	12 762	12 901	13 110	13 254	13 300	13 583
Norway	m. kroner	8 242	9 468	10 956	12 395	12 688	15 446	16 033	18 551	18 865	21 117
Portugal	m. escudos	43 440	51 917	63 817	76 765	92 009	111 375	139 972	159 288	193 864	207 738

Spain	m. pesetas	350 423	400 940	465 695	540 311	594 932	674 883	715 306	852 767	835 353	912 173
Turkey	b. lira	186	313	448	557	803	1 235	1 868	2 477	3 789	6 105
UK	m. pounds	10 923	12 004	14 203	15 605	17 104	18 156	18 581	19 125	19 439	20 803
WTO											
Bulgaria	m. leva	822	874	989	965	1 093	1 127	1 404	1 547	1 751	1 605
Czechoslovakia	m. korunas	21 269	21 349	22 220	23 332	24 387	25 512	26 435	27 362	28 374	28 193
German DR	m. marks	9 875	10 705	11 315	11 970	12 830	13 041	14 045	15 141	15 654	14 871
Hungary	m. forints	17 700	19 060	20 050	21 900	22 700	37 700	38 800	41 500	49 200	49 200
Poland	b. zlotys	74	85	176	191	251	315	466	576	889	2 154
Romania	m. lei	10 394	10 490	11 340	11 662	11 888	12 113	12 208	11 597	11 552	11 753
USSR	m. roubles	:	:	:	:	:	:	:	:	:	:
Other Europe											
Albania	m. leks	899	917	912	888	986	1 700	978	1 055	1 080	1 075
Austria	m. schillings	12 423	12 864	14 140	14 845	15 843	17 875	18 768	18 295	17 650	17 905
Finland	m. markkaa	3 612	4 128	5 182	5 656	6 082	6 555	7 245	7 636	8 419	9 192
Ireland	m. pounds	176	203	241	250	263	283	306	298	303	317
Sweden	m. kronor	15 932	17 467	18 500	19 550	21 164	22 762	24 211	25 662	27 215	29 399
Switzerland	m. francs	3 152	3 349	3 727	3 862	4 009	4 576	4 282	4 203	4 458	4 603
Yugoslavia	b. new dinars	76.3	101	118	155	247	465	979	1 985	5 838	14 600
Middle East											
Bahrain	m. dinars	59.2	80.7	106	62.3	55.6	56.6	60.4	60.3	70.4	70
Cyprus	m. pounds	10.9	17.5	17.9	19.1	19.9	18.5	13.7	16.7	20.4	:
Egypt	m. pounds	:	1 238	1 435	1 801	2 173	2 108	2 493	2 742	2 862	3 462
Iran	b. rials	364	346	341	340	363	455	486	459	505	483
Iraq	m. dinars	990	1 350	2 400	3 200	4 300	4 000	3 600	4 350	4 000	:
Israel	m. new shekels	23.6	53.2	113	309	1 626	4 055	4 936	5 684	6 093	7 373
Jordan	m. dinars	136	160	179	196	197	219	243	253	256	:
Kuwait	m. dinars	257	291	370	416	434	469	430	380	408	438

		1980	1981	1982	1983	1984	1985	1986	1987	1988	1989
Lebanon	m. pounds	980	654	1 215	3 554	2 030	2 448	3 740	..	10 640	..
Oman	m. riyals	407	522	581	670	728	745	665	584	519	510
Saudi Arabia	m. riyals	64 076	75 723	87 695	84 311	77 817	71 992	62 418	60 726	55 750	..
Syria	m. pounds	8 884	9 653	10 703	11 309	12 601	13 000	14 440	14 327	16 638	..
United Arab Emirates	m. dirhams	6 330	7 672	7 268	7 042	7 093	7 500	6 900	5 800	5 800	5 376
Yemen Arab Republic	m. rials	1 978	2 016	2 933	3 104	2 585	2 616	2 808	3 124	5 533	..
Yemen PDR	m. dinars	42.6	56.0	57.5	65.8	67.0	65.3	68.8	72	76	..
South Asia											
Bangladesh	m. taka	2 985	3 210	4 190	5 080	5 325	5 790	7 495	9 080	9 931	11 200
India	m. rupees	38 238	45 371	53 193	61 945	70 834	83 651	105 291	124 965	129 878	131 500
Nepal	m. rupees	242	273	337	430	493	601	866	1 153	1 304	1 565
Pakistan	m. rupees	14 598	17 731	22 637	26 915	30 689	35 110	39 764	43 997	49 991	54 479
Sri Lanka	m. rupees	971	1 051	1 117	1 653	2 194	5 140	7 926	10 103	7 190	7 233
Far East											
Brunei	m. dollars	410	416	480	530	534	617	700	568	..	..
Hong Kong	m. dollars	1 353	1 521	1 478	1 537	1 523	1 639	1 530	1 645	1 676	..
Indonesia	b. new rupiahs	1 708	2 153	2 613	2 858	3 106	2 856	3 089	3 058	3 164	3 378
Japan	b. yen	2 215	2 388	2 532	2 712	2 911	3 118	3 296	3 473	3 655	3 865
Korea, North	m. won	2 750	3 009	3 242	3 530	3 819	3 935	3 976	3 971	3 863	4 060
Korea, South	b. won	2 252	2 831	3 163	3 406	3 573	3 957	4 372	4 915	5 753	6 226
Malaysia	m. ringgits	3 389	4 693	4 975	4 820	4 370	4 320	4 215	6 142	4 160	4 638
Mongolia	m. tugriks	590	630	716	726	764	764	790	837	900	850
Myanmar (Burma)	m. kyats	1 491	1 712	1 643	1 630	1 760	1 973	1 858	1 875	..	..
Philippines	m. pesos	5 829	6 746	7 778	8 530	8 288	7 827	8 662	9 268	10 972	16 447

Country	Unit										
Singapore	m. dollars	1 259	1 507	1 659	1 640	2 204	2 516	2 403	2 439	2 659	2 920
Taiwan	b. dollars	96.5	117	136	139	138	152	158	164	179	186
Thailand	m. baht	34 625	37 375	41 250	45 875	49 500	52 275	51 825	53 125	54 655	57 176
Oceania											
Australia	m. dollars	3 247	3 767	4 371	4 992	5 601	6 298	6 932	7 305	7 535	7 715
Fiji	m. dollars	4.4	3.6	4.2	4.7	4.5	4.5	4.8	9.1	10.3	11.6
New Zealand	m. dollars	426	549	628	656	724	825	1 017	1 211	1 340	1 404
Africa											
Algeria	m. dinars	3 417	3 481	3 893	4 477	4 631	4 793	5 459	5 805	6 070	6 756
Angola	m. kwanzas	15 060	15 060	15 060	23 295	31 943	34 306	34 572	..	26 161	23 438
Benin	m. francs	4 700	5 400	7 821	9 500	9 280	10 190	10 610	9 367	11 420	10 405
Botswana	m. pulas	26.9	28.5	25.2	28.2	34.9	41.7	64.5	124	90.1	..
Burkina Faso	m. francs	7 471	9 216	10 800	11 170	11 780	11 810	17 724	15 241	16 003	..
Burundi	m. francs	2 500	2 700	3 300	3 200	3 900	4 200	4 780	3 910	3 198	4 414
Cameroon	m. francs	19 540	21 415	41 015	63 105	73 658	81 920	86 905	83 150	77 889	50 000
Central African Rep.	m. francs	2 816	4 029	5 000	6 500	6 500	6 189	5 892	5 610	..	..
Chad	m. francs	..	..	..	15 000	17 496	17 000	16 850	10 307	20 000	..
Congo	m. francs	10 050	11 250	16 500	18 600	21 596	25 000	25 625	26 200	20 440	23 580
Côte d'Ivoire	m. francs	26 643	25 000	28 400	29 658	30 706	31 320	33 547	35 336	36 250	37 193
Ethiopia	m. birr	744	760	802	845	897	923	972	1 182	1 407	1 687
Gabon	m. francs	18 600	25 600	29 100	33 000	35 100	42 900	47 100	43 407	40 000	40 680
Ghana	m. cedis	175	488	587	894	1 605	3 432	4 605	6 659	4 603	8 028
Kenya	m. shillings	2 016	2 182	2 662	2 778	2 523	2 395	3 342	3 909	3 945	4 328
Liberia	m. dollars	27.1	51.6	46.9	25.3	25.2	24.4	23.0	25.8	27.4	..
Libya	m. dinars	1 058	1 310	1 330	1 107	1 096	1 096	819	549	582	..
Madagascar	m. francs	19 315	23 500	27 200	29 600	31 730	33 520	39 830	39 200	39 200	..
Malawi	m. kwachas	43.2	36.0	29.0	26.1	26.6	28.6	46.1	47.8	61.6	71.5
Mali	m. francs	8 100	8 600	9 700	10 200	11 100	13 400	13 000	13 300	12 300	23 000

		1980	1981	1982	1983	1984	1985	1986	1987	1988	1989
Mauritania	m. ouguiyas	3 700	3 293	2 931	2 639	..	..	..	..	..	..
Mauritius	m. rupees	42.6	47.7	30.8	34.4	36.5	36.1	36.3	38.5	64.9	81.8
Morocco	m. dirhams	4 400	5 047	5 814	4 675	4 960	6 453	6 837	7 190	7 630	..
Mozambique	m. meticais	4 419	5 741	6 900	8 300	10 300	10 300	11 214	29 600	50 400	80 000
Niger	m. francs	3 867	4 286	4 232	4 389	4 775	5 075	5 325	5 175	..	..
Nigeria	m. nairas	1 352	1 319	1 113	1 179	928	976	957	810	1 270	1 034
Rwanda	m. francs	2 027	2 500	2 622	2 693	2 500	2 760	3 050	2 979	2 800	..
Senegal	m. francs	19 870	21 565	23 505	25 110	27 046	28 235	28 490	28 784	29 630	28 476
Sierra Leone	m. leones	14.1	17.5	17.9	18.6	23.3	29.4	64.5	101	125	161
Somalia	m. shillings	601	824	826	1 300	1 786	1 751	2 300	3 800	3 500	..
South Africa	m. rands	2 419	2 615	2 967	3 314	3 922	4 414	5 412	6 717	7 835	9 873
Sudan	m. pounds	132	131	139	212	361	468	562	723	968	1 831
Swaziland	m. emalangeni	10.9	12.0	16.2	16.0	16.1	15.7	15.9	16.8	21.5	24.0
Tanzania	m. shillings	1 688	2 122	2 433	2 651	3 201	4 277	7 073	11 025	16 250	21 574
Togo	m. francs	5 155	6 202	6 138	6 328	7 007	8 632	9 200	13 047	13 047	13 765
Tunisia	m. dinars	78.6	113	284	364	296	357	413	434	460	460
Uganda	m. shillings	29.6	54.1	82.3	144	327	782	1 157	4 805	8 500	460
Zaire	m. zaires	430	316	873	723	1 928	2 013	2 700	5 000	6 500	14 869
Zambia	m. kwachas	106	154	148	161	148	167	480	637	717	896
Zimbabwe	m. dollars	243	284	296	353	398	436	554	661	720	804
Central America											
Costa Rica	m. colones	265	317	528	928	1 140	1 202	1 426	1 504	1 586	1 660
Cuba	m. pesos	973	1 011	1 109	1 133	1 386	1 335	1 307	1 300	1 350	1 377
Dominican Rep.	m. pesos	99	126	128	129	164	191	202	250	298	346
El Salvador	m. colones	254	322	395	442	534	630	964	885	..	..
Guatemala	m. quetzales	143	161	208	231	270	371	378	495	645	731
Haiti	m. gourdes	100	105	104	102	110	131	138	150	..	..
Honduras	m. lempiras	120	125	160	240	335	445	450	450	..	..

Jamaica	m. dollars	62.0	81.8	98.8	97.8	104	124	125	125	..	1 673
Mexico	b. pesos	24.7	37.9	47.4	90.3	181	297	470	894	1 470	77 721
Nicaragua	m. cordobas	1	1.3	1.7	3.4	4.9	26.8	91	921	93 827	
Panama	m. balboas	42.2	46.5	55.0	60.0	88.0	92.0	105	105	113	76
Trinidad and Tobago	m. dollars	296	371	563	545	490	465	465	..	..	..
South America											
Argentina	m. australes	1.8	3.9	8.9	31.2	236	1 387	2 727	5 863	28 224	300 000
Bolivia	t. bolivianos	4.8	8.0	19.0	58.0	721	94 677	299 374	327 547	400 300	489 214
Brazil	b. cruzados	0.2	0.3	0.8	1.4	4.7	16	45	131	1 023	7 458
Chile	m. pesos	72 525	94 810	117 831	124 901	182 203	194 877	258 675	277 417	385 145	446 768
Colombia	m. pesos	29 023	35 830	44 661	69 531	91 753	105 092	135 712	176 989	265 484	398 226
Ecuador	m. sucres	5 213	5 848	6 870	8 833	12 086	19 743	25 598	35 442	52 595	83 839
Guyana	m. dollars	98	96	108	142	156	192	276	..	..	..
Paraguay	m. guaranies	7 644	10 581	11 566	11 676	12 826	15 937	20 097	26 885	32 643	57 978
Peru	m. intis	265	515	1 480	2 530	3 875	11 900	23 900	37 000	103 842	800 000
Uruguay	m. new pesos	2 693	4 770	5 168	5 877	7 708	12 831	22 828	36 831	59 962	..
Venezuela	m. bolivares	6 899	8 952	9 905	8 488	9 800	9 457	10 520	15 197	17 585	21 049

Table A2. World military expenditure, in constant price figures, 1980–89

Figures are in US $m., at 1988 prices and exchange-rates.

	1980	1981	1982	1983	1984	1985	1986	1987	1988	1989
NATO										
North America										
Canada	7 230	7 353	8 077	8 534	9 093	9 362	9 535	9 747	9 897	9 928
USA	206 573	220 955	240 616	258 828	270 923	290 026	305 076	300 890	294 901	289 139
Europe										
Belgium	4 614	4 657	4 502	4 323	4 139	4 092	4 261	4 287	4 107	4 116
Denmark	2 235	2 260	2 323	2 342	2 287	2 234	2 153	2 275	2 320	2 245
France	32 222	32 995	33 668	34 252	34 104	34 103	35 118	36 137	36 105	36 410
FR Germany	33 807	34 216	33 786	34 054	33 712	33 796	34 719	35 320	35 097	34 955
Greece	2 841	3 360	3 428	3 128	3 717	3 688	3 152	3 144	3 378	3 286
Italy	14 174	14 269	15 262	15 585	16 057	16 634	16 964	19 199	20 429	20 821
Luxembourg	60	62	63	64	64	63	66	75	86	83
Netherlands	6 510	6 575	6 555	6 497	6 608	6 533	6 633	6 753	6 729	6 811
Norway	2 422	2 447	2 545	2 656	2 558	2 946	2 853	3 037	2 895	3 101
Portugal	1 145	1 142	1 142	1 099	1 021	1 036	1 166	1 213	1 347	1 299
Spain	6 423	6 413	6 518	6 738	6 669	6 952	6 772	7 672	7 171	7 434
Turkey	1 876	2 316	2 528	2 393	2 325	2 467	2 772	2 647	2 664	2 715
UK	31 100	30 549	33 283	34 981	36 511	36 548	36 173	35 713	34 629	34 466
EC	135 656	137 000	141 039	143 541	145 352	146 151	147 669	152 253	151 860	152 388
WTO										
Bulgaria	678	718	810	780	877	800	1 071	1 180	1 337	1 225
Czechoslovakia	3 491	3 473	3 454	3 589	3 716	3 838	3 962	4 097	4 241	4 207
German DR	4 685	5 068	5 357	5 667	6 075	6 181	6 656	7 176	7 419	7 048

Hungary	1 551	1 597	1 571	1 599	1 531	2 375	2 321	2 285	2 343	2 006
Poland	4 389	4 117	4 262	3 796	4 332	4 730	5 945	5 863	5 657	5 431
Romania	1 597	1 578	1 458	1 425	1 437	1 470	1 483	1 407	1 402	1 426
USSR	. .	. .	. .	. .	. .	. .	. .	. .	. .	. .
Other Europe										
Albania	150	153	152	148	164	283	163	176	180	179
Austria	1 342	1 300	1 355	1 378	1 392	1 521	1 571	1 510	1 429	1 410
Finland	1 467	1 496	1 714	1 726	1 733	1 765	1 895	1 919	2 013	2 054
Ireland	525	502	509	478	463	472	492	465	462	462
Sweden	4 596	4 539	4 380	4 253	4 263	4 258	4 357	4 431	4 442	4 504
Switzerland	2 765	2 761	2 907	2 926	2 949	3 255	3 022	2 926	3 047	3 055
Yugoslavia	2 571	2 431	2 151	2 019	2 080	2 272	2 520	2 314	2 314	. .
Middle East										
Bahrain	185	226	273	156	139	145	158	161	187	186
Cyprus	35	50	48	49	48	43	31	37	44	. .
Egypt	. .	5 392	5 442	5 889	6 070	5 252	5 013	4 607	4 089	4 222
Iran	16 108	12 321	10 230	8 523	8 082	9 705	9 339	7 679	7 353	. .
Iraq	12 306	14 007	21 952	28 596	31 590	23 506	16 531	17 073	12 868	. .
Israel	6 110	6 887	7 314	8 000	8 420	5 249	4 318	4 134	3 811	3 849
Jordan	490	535	557	581	562	607	673	703	689	. .
Kuwait	1 181	1 246	1 470	1 579	1 629	1 733	1 574	1 382	1 463	1 529
Lebanon	102	59	96	262	107	93	97	. .	26	. .
Oman	691	859	1 016	1 296	1 478	1 517	1 730	1 189	1 350	1 326
Saudi Arabia	16 114	18 557	21 614	20 899	19 513	18 666	16 684	16 384	14 887	. .
Syria	3 960	3 635	3 526	3 511	3 582	3 152	2 573	1 601	1 482	. .
United Arab Emirates	1 847	2 088	1 955	1 966	2 091	2 211	2 004	1 587	1 580	1 454
Yemen Arab Republic	332	322	456	457	339	323	325	340	566	. .
Yemen PDR	197	249	234	241	243	225	224	221	220	. .

	1980	1981	1982	1983	1984	1985	1986	1987	1988	1989
South Asia										
Bangladesh	219	203	235	261	247	243	283	313	313	311
India	5 547	5 819	6 325	6 582	6 955	7 778	9 006	9 822	9 332	9 030
Nepal	23	23	26	29	33	37	45	54	56	62
Pakistan	1 350	1 466	1 767	1 974	2 122	2 299	2 516	2 658	2 777	2 803
Sri Lanka	71	65	63	82	93	214	306	362	226	205
Far East										
Brunei	263	245	265	290	283	319	356	287	..	..
Hong Kong	313	309	271	256	235	245	223	226	215	..
Indonesia	2 012	2 596	2 505	2 451	2 410	2 116	2 163	1 960	1 877	1 876
Japan	20 099	20 628	21 291	22 400	23 504	24 672	25 924	27 289	28 521	29 350
Korea, North	1 279	1 400	1 508	1 642	1 776	1 830	1 849	1 847	1 797	1 888
Korea, South	4 924	5 103	5 318	5 535	5 675	6 135	6 593	7 195	7 865	8 030
Malaysia	1 689	2 132	2 129	1 990	1 742	1 716	1 664	2 406	1 589	1 725
Mongolia	197	210	239	242	255	255	263	279	300	283
Myanmar (Burma)	461	528	481	452	465	488	421	340	..	..
Philippines	797	815	854	851	550	422	463	478	520	708
Singapore	739	816	866	845	1 107	1 258	1 218	1 230	1 321	1 414
Taiwan	4 460	4 432	5 000	5 043	5 007	5 526	5 704	5 891	6 348	6 346
Thailand	1 886	1 808	1 895	2 031	2 174	2 240	2 182	2 181	2 161	2 160
Oceania										
Australia	4 827	5 070	5 309	5 524	5 934	6 272	5 334	6 166	5 910	5 692
Fiji	5	4	4	4	4	4	4	7	7	8
New Zealand	687	768	756	735	765	754	822	845	879	879
Africa										
Algeria	1 144	1 016	1 066	1 138	1 107	1 036	1 050	1 040	1 026	1 047

Angola	502	502	502	777	1 065	1 144	1 152	..	872	781
Benin	34	29	40	44	41	43	43	35	38	32
Botswana	33	30	24	24	27	30	42	75	50	..
Burkina Faso	36	42	43	41	42	39	60	53	54	..
Burundi	31	30	34	31	33	34	38	29	23	23
Cameroon	134	133	225	296	311	341	336	303	262	154
Central African Rep.	14	18	20	23	22	19	18	18	..	..
Chad	..	..	..	61	59	54	62	39	67	..
Congo	62	60	78	81	84	91	91	91	69	76
Côte d'Ivoire	135	117	124	122	121	121	121	127	122	123
Ethiopia	488	469	475	496	486	420	490	611	680	780
Gabon	93	117	114	117	118	134	139	129	134	142
Ghana	18	23	23	16	20	39	42	44	23	35
Kenya	251	243	247	231	190	160	214	238	222	222
Liberia	38	67	58	30	30	29	26	28	27	..
Libya	3 596	4 452	4 520	3 762	3 725	3 725	2 784	1 866	1 978	..
Madagascar	53	50	44	40	39	37	39	33	28	..
Malawi	60	44	33	26	22	21	30	25	24	25
Mali	38	39	42	42	44	51	47	47	41	74
Mauritania	95	71	56	50	..	..	..	..	..	..
Mauritius	5.5	5.3	3.1	3.3	3.2	3.0	3.0	3.1	4.8	5.4
Morocco	980	999	1 042	788	744	898	876	896	929	..
Mozambique	59	61	58	55	53	42	36	75	101	126
Niger	17	15	13	14	14	15	16	17	..	..
Nigeria	1 134	914	717	616	347	346	322	248	281	..
Rwanda	38	45	42	40	35	38	43	40	37	..
Senegal	117	120	111	106	103	95	90	95	100	..
Sierra Leone	24	24	19	12	8.9	6.4	7.7	4.3	4.0	4.1
Somalia	64	60	49	57	41	29	28	36	21	..
South Africa	3 206	3 003	2 970	2 956	3 137	3 036	3 139	3 355	3 468	3 802

	1980	1981	1982	1983	1984	1985	1986	1987	1988	1989
Sudan	242	194	163	191	242	216	208	239	215	272
Swaziland	14	13	15	13	12	9.7	8.8	8.3	9.5	9.5
Tanzania	143	144	127	109	98	97	121	146	164	170
Togo	25	25	22	21	24	30	31	44	44	46
Tunisia	175	231	509	599	449	502	549	538	536	501
Uganda	72	82	83	116	185	190	104	128	80	..
Zaire	62	34	69	32	57	48	44	46	35	53
Zambia	110	140	120	109	84	69	130	121	87	83
Zimbabwe	374	387	364	353	331	334	371	394	400	393
Central America										
Costa Rica	25	21	19	25	27	25	27	24	21	19
Cuba	1 254	1 303	1 429	1 460	1 786	1 721	1 685	1 676	1 740	1 775
Dominican Republic	62	73	69	66	66	56	54	58	49	..
El Salvador	199	219	241	238	258	249	288	212	..	258
Guatemala	134	135	174	184	208	241	180	209	246	..
Haiti	29	28	26	23	23	25	25	31	..	..
Honduras	94	89	105	145	194	249	241	235	..	..
Jamaica	32	38	43	38	32	30	26	25	..	..
Mexico	1 080	1 296	1 015	959	1 161	1 208	1 027	842	647	615
Nicaragua	265	279	292	445	473	810	352	352	348	..
Panama	50	51	58	62	90	93	106	105	113	76
Trinidad and Tobago	177	194	264	222	176	155	144	..	..	..
South America										
Argentina	5 414	5 711	4 927	3 897	4 056	3 087	3 194	2 966	3 225	3 000
Bolivia	170	243	238	202	182	201	169	162	170	..
Brazil	4 609	3 362	4 532	3 276	3 703	3 857	4 428	3 908	3 899	3 691
Chile	1 276	1 394	1 574	1 313	1 597	1 307	1 451	1 299	1 572	1 568

Colombia	499	484	483	629	715	660	716	758	887	1 053
Ecuador	147	142	143	124	129	165	174	186	174	158
Guyana	47	37	34	40	35	37	50	:	:	:
Paraguay	57	69	71	63	58	57	55	60	59	59
Peru	422	492	785	671	487	568	641	534	806	6 21
Uruguay	223	294	268	205	173	167	169	166	167	:
Venezuela	1 489	1 663	1 678	1 354	1 392	1 207	1 204	1 357	1 213	7 52

Table A3. World military expenditure as a percentage of gross domestic product, 1979–88

	1979	1980	1981	1982	1983	1984	1985	1986	1987	1988
NATO										
North America										
Canada	1.7	1.8	1.8	2.0	2.1	2.1	2.1	2.1	2.1	2.0
USA	5.0	5.4	5.7	6.3	6.5	6.4	6.6	6.7	6.4	6.1
Europe										
Belgium	3.3	3.3	3.4	3.3	3.2	3.1	3.0	3.0	2.9	2.7
Denmark	2.3	2.4	2.5	2.5	2.5	2.3	2.2	2.0	2.1	2.2
France	3.9	4.0	4.1	4.1	4.1	4.0	4.0	3.9	4.0	3.8
FR Germany	3.3	3.3	3.4	3.4	3.4	3.3	3.2	3.1	3.1	2.9
Greece	6.3	5.7	7.0	6.8	6.3	7.1	7.0	6.2	6.3	6.4
Italy	2.4	2.1	2.1	2.3	2.3	2.3	2.3	2.2	2.4	2.5
Luxembourg	0.9	1.0	1.1	1.0	1.1	1.0	0.9	0.9	1.1	1.1
Netherlands	3.2	3.1	3.2	3.2	3.2	3.2	3.1	3.1	3.1	3.0
Norway	3.1	2.9	2.9	3.0	3.1	2.8	3.1	3.1	3.3	3.2
Portugal	3.5	3.5	3.5	3.5	3.3	3.3	3.1	3.2	3.1	3.2
Spain	2.1	2.3	2.4	2.4	2.4	2.4	2.4	2.2	2.4	2.1
Turkey	4.3	4.3	4.9	5.2	4.8	4.4	4.5	4.8	4.2	3.8
UK	4.4	4.7	4.7	5.1	5.1	5.3	5.1	4.9	4.6	4.3
WTO										
Bulgaria	3.1	3.0	3.0	3.3	3.1	3.3	3.4	4.0	4.2	4.4
Czechoslovakia	3.2	3.1	3.1	3.1	3.2	3.3	3.3	3.4	3.4	3.4
German DR	4.1	4.2	4.4	4.5	4.5	4.7	4.6	4.8	5.0	5.0
Hungary	2.4	2.5	2.4	2.4	2.4	2.3	3.6	3.6	3.4	3.5
Poland	2.9	3.0	3.1	3.2	2.8	2.9	3.0	3.6	3.4	3.0
Romania	2.0	1.7	1.6	1.5	1.5	1.4	1.4	1.3	1.2	1.2

USSR	:	:	:	:	:	:	:	:	:	:
Other Europe										
Austria	1.3	1.2	1.2	1.2	1.2	1.2	1.3	1.3	1.2	1.1
Finland	1.8	1.9	1.9	2.1	2.1	2.0	1.9	2.0	1.9	1.9
Ireland	1.8	1.9	1.8	1.8	1.7	1.6	1.6	1.6	1.5	1.4
Sweden	3.1	3.0	3.0	2.9	2.8	2.7	2.6	2.6	2.6	2.5
Switzerland	1.9	1.9	1.8	1.9	1.9	1.9	2.0	1.8	1.7	1.7
Yugoslavia	4.7	4.9	4.6	4.0	3.8	3.7	3.9	3.9	3.6	3.6
Middle East										
Bahrain	5.3	4.8	5.9	7.5	4.3	3.8	4.2	5.1	5.3	5.0
Cyprus	2.0	1.4	2.0	1.7	1.7	1.5	1.2	0.9	0.9	1.0
Egypt	2.9	:	6.5	6.3	6.7	6.9	5.8	6.1	6.2	:
Iran	6.3	5.4	4.3	3.4	2.6	2.5	3.0	:	:	:
Iraq	6.9	6.3	12.3	19.0	24.4	29.1	27.5	:	:	:
Israel	26.1	25.0	23.5	19.0	20.2	21.4	14.4	11.3	10.2	9.1
Jordan	17.7	13.8	13.7	13.5	13.8	13.1	13.6	14.8	15.0	15.0
Kuwait	3.3	3.5	4.4	6.0	6.8	6.8	7.9	8.6	7.0	7.3
Lebanon	4.1	4.1	2.4	4.3	12.0	:	:	:	:	:
Oman	20.9	19.7	21.0	22.2	24.5	23.9	21.6	23.8	17.6	:
Saudi Arabia	21.1	16.6	14.5	21.1	20.3	20.9	22.0	22.4	22.7	:
Syria	16.0	17.3	14.7	15.6	15.4	16.7	15.6	14.4	11.3	:
United Arab Emirates	5.5	5.8	6.3	6.5	6.8	7.0	7.6	8.7	6.7	6.6
Yemen Arab Republic	20.9	15.0	12.6	14.7	14.2	10.4	8.4	7.3	7.2	:
Yemen PDR	17.5	17.8	19.7	18.7	19.1	17.7	16.7	:	:	:
South Asia										
Bangladesh	1.3	1.4	1.3	1.5	1.6	1.4	1.3	1.5	1.6	:
India	3.5	3.0	3.0	3.1	3.1	3.2	3.3	3.7	3.9	3.7

	1979	1980	1981	1982	1983	1984	1985	1986	1987	1988
Nepal	1.0	1.0	0.9	1.1	1.2	1.2	1.3	1.6	1.8	2.2
Pakistan	5.6	5.7	5.9	6.6	6.9	6.8	6.8	7.3	7.1	6.9
Sri Lanka	1.5	1.5	1.2	1.1	1.4	1.4	3.2	4.4	5.1	3.2
Far East										
Brunei	6.1	3.9	4.5	5.3	6.5	6.5	7.7	:	:	:
Hong Kong	0.6	1.0	0.9	0.8	0.7	0.6	0.6	0.5	0.5	0.4
Indonesia	4.1	3.8	3.7	4.2	3.7	3.5	3.0	3.0	2.5	2.3
Japan	0.9	0.9	0.9	0.9	1.0	1.0	1.0	1.0	1.0	1.0
Korea, North	10.4	10.7	11.5	11.8	12.3	12.0	:	:	9.5	8.7
Korea, South	5.1	5.9	6.0	5.8	5.3	4.9	4.9	4.7	4.5	4.6
Malaysia	5.5	6.4	8.1	7.9	6.9	5.5	5.6	5.9	6.1	6.3
Mongolia	:	:	:	:	:	:	11.2	11.0	11.3	11.7
Myanmar (Burma)	3.8	3.9	4.1	3.6	3.3	3.3	3.6	3.2	:	:
Philippines	2.4	2.2	2.2	2.3	2.2	1.5	1.3	1.4	1.3	1.3
Singapore	5.0	5.0	5.1	5.1	4.5	5.5	6.5	6.3	5.8	5.5
Taiwan	6.8	6.6	6.7	7.3	6.8	6.1	6.4	5.9	6.3	6.0
Thailand	5.4	5.1	4.8	4.9	5.0	5.0	5.0	4.7	4.3	4.0
Oceania										
Australia	2.4	2.6	2.6	2.7	2.8	2.8	2.8	2.8	2.6	2.4
Fiji	0.4	0.4	0.3	0.4	0.4	0.4	0.3	0.3	0.6	0.7
New Zealand	1.8	1.9	2.1	2.1	2.0	1.9	1.9	2.0	2.0	2.1
Africa										
Algeria	2.1	2.1	1.8	1.9	1.9	1.8	1.7	1.7	1.7	1.5
Angola	14.0	12.8	13.8	11.9	16.5	22.0	28.4	28.4	:	21.5
Benin	1.9	1.9	1.8	1.9	2.2	2.0	2.0	1.9	:	:
Botswana	3.6	3.7	3.7	2.7	2.4	2.4	2.1	2.7	4.2	2.7
Burkina Faso	2.7	2.7	2.8	3.0	2.9	3.0	2.5	3.5	3.0	:

Burundi	2.6	2.9	3.0	3.5	3.1	3.2	3.0	3.4	2.7	2.2
Cameroon	1.5	1.2	1.1	1.7	2.2	2.1	2.2	2.1	2.1	:
Central African Rep.	2.0	1.7	2.1	2.0	2.6	2.3	2.0	1.8	1.7	:
Chad	:	:	:	:	7.0	7.8	5.7	6.0	3.8	:
Congo	3.7	2.8	2.1	2.3	2.3	2.3	2.6	4.0	:	:
Côte d'Ivoire	1.1	1.2	1.1	1.1	1.1	1.1	1.0	1.0	1.2	:
Ethiopia	8.8	8.5	8.4	8.4	8.6	9.0	8.9	8.9	10.6	10.0
Gabon	1.9	2.1	2.4	2.4	2.6	2.3	2.6	4.0	4.3	3.9
Ghana	0.5	0.4	0.7	0.7	0.5	0.6	1.0	0.9	0.9	0.5
Kenya	4.4	3.8	3.6	3.8	3.6	2.9	2.4	2.9	3.0	2.6
Liberia	1.5	2.8	4.8	4.3	2.3	2.4	2.3	2.2	:	:
Libya	14.2	10.0	14.0	15.0	13.0	14.5	15.2	12.7	:	:
Madagascar	2.9	2.8	3.0	2.7	2.4	2.3	2.2	2.2	1.8	:
Malawi	4.2	4.4	3.3	2.4	1.9	1.6	1.5	1.8	1.6	:
Mali	:	2.3	2.3	2.4	2.4	2.4	2.7	2.3	:	:
Mauritania	10.5	9.7	7.6	6.9	5.7	:	:	:	:	:
Mauritius	0.2	0.5	0.4	0.3	0.3	0.2	0.2	0.2	0.2	0.2
Morocco	5.6	6.3	6.6	6.5	4.9	4.7	5.4	5.1	5.0	5.0
Mozambique	:	5.6	7.0	8.0	10.7	12.1	11.7	10.4	:	:
Niger	0.7	0.7	0.7	0.6	0.7	0.7	0.7	0.8	0.8	:
Nigeria	2.5	2.5	2.3	1.8	1.9	1.3	1.2	1.2	0.7	0.9
Rwanda	1.8	1.9	2.0	2.0	1.9	1.6	1.6	1.9	:	:
Senegal	3.3	3.1	2.8	2.8	2.7	2.7	2.5	2.2	2.0	:
Sierra Leone	0.7	1.0	1.0	0.8	0.7	0.7	0.6	1.1	:	:
Somalia	6.8	4.9	4.3	3.4	3.8	2.7	1.8	1.8	1.8	:
South Africa	4.3	3.9	3.7	3.7	3.7	3.7	3.7	3.7	4.0	3.9
Sudan	2.0	2.3	2.0	1.7	2.1	2.9	2.6	2.1	:	:
Swaziland	2.3	2.1	2.2	2.9	2.6	2.3	1.8	1.7	:	:
Tanzania	7.6	4.0	4.3	4.2	3.9	3.8	3.8	4.7	4.7	:
Togo	2.2	2.2	2.4	2.3	2.2	2.3	2.6	2.5	2.6	:

	1979	1980	1981	1982	1983	1984	1985	1986	1987	1988
Tunisia	2.2	2.2	2.7	5.9	6.6	4.7	5.2	5.9	5.5	5.3
Uganda	1.3	2.2	3.8	2.7	3.0	5.0	5.9	3.8	3.5	:
Zaire	3.0	2.5	1.3	2.8	1.2	1.9	1.4	1.3	1.5	1.5
Zambia	4.8	3.5	4.4	4.1	3.9	3.0	2.4	3.7	3.2	3.2
Zimbabwe	6.0	7.1	6.4	5.7	5.7	6.2	5.7	6.2	6.5	5.8
Central America										
Costa Rica	0.6	0.6	0.6	0.5	0.7	0.7	0.6	0.6	0.5	0.4
Cuba	10.5	9.9	8.8	9.1	8.8	10.1	9.6	10.2	10.7	11.3
Dominican Republic	2.0	1.5	1.7	1.6	1.5	1.6	1.4	1.3	1.3	1.1
El Salvador	1.8	2.8	3.7	4.4	4.4	4.6	4.4	4.9	3.8	:
Guatemala	1.7	1.8	1.9	2.3	2.6	2.9	3.3	2.4	2.8	3.2
Haiti	1.4	1.4	1.4	1.3	1.2	1.1	1.2	1.4	:	:
Honduras	2.2	2.4	2.3	2.8	4.0	5.2	6.4	6.0	5.5	:
Jamaica	0.9	1.3	1.6	1.7	1.4	1.1	1.1	0.9	0.8	:
Mexico	0.6	0.6	0.6	0.5	0.5	0.6	0.7	0.6	0.5	:
Nicaragua	3.1	4.4	5.3	6.0	10.3	10.9	23.2	20.9	34.2	:
Panama	1.5	1.2	1.2	1.3	1.4	1.9	1.9	2.0	2.0	2.5
Trinidad and Tobago	1.9	2.0	2.3	2.9	2.9	2.6	2.6	2.7	:	:
South America										
Argentina	6.3	6.4	7.1	6.0	4.6	4.5	3.5	3.7	3.4	3.0
Bolivia	3.6	4.0	5.3	4.5	3.9	3.4	3.4	2.8	2.9	3.1
Brazil	0.9	1.3	1.3	1.6	1.2	1.2	1.1	1.2	1.1	1.1
Chile	7.0	6.7	7.4	9.5	8.0	9.6	7.6	8.0	6.8	7.8
Colombia	1.7	1.8	1.8	1.8	2.3	2.4	2.1	2.0	2.0	2.3
Ecuador	2.0	1.8	1.7	1.7	1.6	1.5	1.8	1.9	2.0	1.7
Guyana	5.1	6.5	6.0	7.5	9.7	9.2	9.8	12.4	:	:
Paraguay	1.3	1.4	1.5	1.6	1.4	1.2	1.1	1.1	1.1	1.0

Peru	3.9	5.3	6.0	8.5	8.1	5.6	6.4	6.6	5.0	2.5
Uruguay	2.4	2.9	3.9	4.0	3.2	2.6	2.4	2.3	2.1	2.1
Venezuela	2.4	2.7	3.1	3.4	2.9	2.4	2.0	2.1	2.1	1.9

Table A1: Military expenditure figures are given in local currency at current prices. Figures for recent years are budget estimates.

Table A2: This series is based on the data given in the local currency series, deflated to 1988 price levels and converted into dollars at 1988 period-average exchange-rates. Local consumer price indices (CPI) are taken as far as possible from *International Financial Statistics* (IFS) (International Monetary Fund: Washington, DC). For the most recent year, the CPI is an estimate based on the first 6–10 months of the year. For a few countries, where CPI is not available, current prices are used. Period-average exchange-rates are taken as far as possible from the IFS. For WTO countries, purchasing power parities (PPP) are used.

Table A3: The share of gross domestic product (GDP) is calculated in local currency. GDP data are taken as far as possible from the IFS. For some socialist economies, gross national product (GNP) or net material product (NMP) is used.

Appendix B. Sources and methods

I. Methods and definitions

Since the publication of the first *SIPRI Yearbook*,[1] SIPRI has provided annual 10-year time series data on world military expenditure. The main purpose of the data is to provide an easily identifiable measure, over time, of the scale of resources absorbed by the military in various countries. Expenditure data are only indirectly related to military strength, although changes in the data over time can be utilized to measure governments' perception of military capability.

In recent years, the information available on world military expenditure has increased in quantitative terms, while there has been a decline in the quality of information provided. Although here are now many more sources, the available data has become less reliable. In addition to the primary sources of national budgets and documents published by international organizations, the military expenditure project also studies over 50 specialist journals, annual reference volumes and newspapers.

The NATO definition of military expenditure is utilized as a guide-line. Where possible, the following items are included: all current and capital expenditure on the armed forces, in the running of defence departments and other government agencies engaged in defence projects as well as space projects; the cost of paramilitary forces and police when judged to be trained and equipped for military operations; military R&D, tests and evaluation costs; and costs of retirement pensions of service personnel, including pensions of civilian employees. Military aid is included in the expenditure of the donor countries. Excluded are items on civil defence, interest on war debts and veteran's payments. Calendar year figures are calculated from fiscal year data where necessary, on the assumption that expenditure takes place evenly throughout the year.

It must be emphasized that all military expenditure data for recent years are estimates with some degree of uncertainty. This applies in particular to data for Eastern Europe which, in light of recent changes, are currently being revised. The present data should be considered provisional. In this context it should be noted that SIPRI is currently producing a detailed research report on the methodology and quality of all military expenditure data, which will contain more information than is possible here. This is expected to be a major benefit to researchers who wish to do country and

---

[1] *SIPRI Yearbook of World Armaments and Disarmament 1968/69* (Almqvist & Wiksell: Stockholm, 1969). See also the *SIPRI Yearbooks 1969* through *1990*.

regional studies based on military expenditure data; the report will be available at the end of 1990, and readers are requested to write to SIPRI to acquire a copy. It should be stressed that even though SIPRI provides military expenditure in constant prices, it does not encourage close comparison between individual countries. Priority is given to the choice of providing a uniform definition *over time for each country* to show a correct time trend, rather than to adjusting the figures for single years according to the common definition. In addition, the recent phenomenon of violently fluctuating exchange-rates (and their lack of correlation to inflationary differentials) makes common dollar figures more difficult to compare. In the absence of explicit military prices, obeying purchasing power parity, the present system must therefore be kept.[2]

II. Main sources of military expenditure data

Estimates of military expenditure are made on the basis of national sources, including budgets, White Papers and statistical documents published by the government or the central bank of the country concerned. The reference publications listed below are also used. Journals and newspapers are consulted for the most recent figures.

NATO

Financial and Economic Data Relating to NATO Defence, annual press release (NATO: Brussels)

Non-Soviet WTO

Alton, T. P., Lazaricik, G., Bass, E. M. and Badach, K., 'East European defense expenditures, 1965–1982', *East European Economies: Slow Growth in the 1980s*, vol. 2: *Economic Performance and Policy*, selected papers submitted to the Joint Economic Committee, US Congress (US Government Printing Office: Washington, DC, 1985)

Annual reference publications

Government Finance Statistics Yearbook (International Monetary Fund: Washington, DC)
Statistical Yearbook (United Nations: New York)
Statistical Yearbook for Asia and the Pacific (United Nations: Bangkok)
Statistik des Auslandes (Federal Statistical Office: Wiesbaden)
Europa Yearbook (Europa Publications: London)
The Military Balance (International Institute for Strategic Studies: London)

---

[2] For an earlier discussion of methodology, see SIPRI, *World Armaments and Disarmament: SIPRI Yearbook 1984* (Taylor & Francis: London and Philadelphia, 1984), appendix 3B, pp. 132–36.

INDEX